Donated to the library through a generous gift

to

Book Funds

from

Anonymous

WHEN THE
LAND WAS
YOUNG

ALSO BY SHARMAN APT RUSSELL

Kill the Cowboy:
A Battle of Mythology in
the New West

Songs of the Fluteplayer

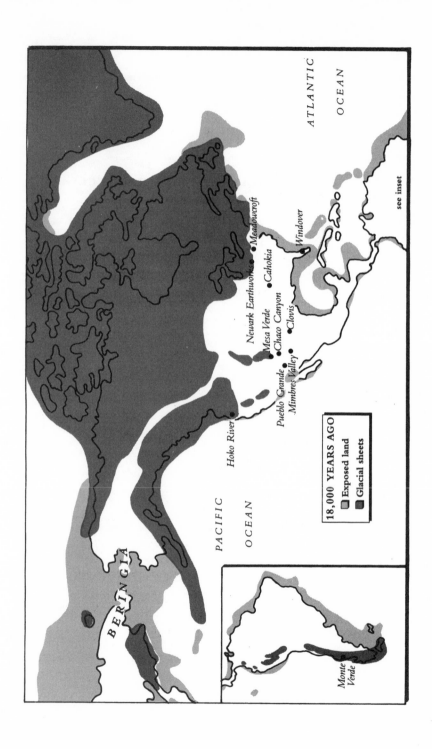

ATLANTIC OCEAN

see inset

Meadowcroft

Newark Earthworks

Cahokia

Windover

Mesa Verde

Chaco Canyon

Clovis

Mimbres Valley

Pueblo Grande

Hoko River

PACIFIC OCEAN

18,000 YEARS AGO
■ Exposed land
■ Glacial sheets

BERINGIA

Monte Verde

WHEN THE LAND WAS YOUNG

Reflections on
American Archaeology

SHARMAN APT RUSSELL

ADDISON-WESLEY PUBLISHING COMPANY, INC.
*Reading, Massachusetts   Menlo Park, California   New York
Don Mills, Ontario   Harlow, England   Amsterdam   Bonn
Sydney   Singapore   Tokyo   Madrid   San Juan
Paris   Seoul   Milan   Mexico City   Taipei*

Grateful acknowledgment is made to Simon & Schuster for permission to reprint material from *Cabeza de Vaca's Adventures into the Unknown Interior of America,* edited by Cyclone Covey (New York, Macmillan, 1961).

Library of Congress Cataloging-in-Publication Data

Russell, Sharman Apt.
    When the land was young : reflections on American archaeology / Sharman Apt Russell.
      p. cm.
    Includes bibliographical references and index.
    ISBN 0-201-40698-5
    1. Indians of North America—Antiquities.   2. Archaeology—North America—History.   3. North America—Antiquities.   I. Title.
E77.9.R87   1996
970.01—dc20   95-48491
                                                             CIP

Jacket design by Suzanne Heiser
Text design, map, and timeline by Karen Savary
Set in 12-point Bembo by Shepard Poorman Communications Corp.

1 2 3 4 5 6 7 8 9-DOH-0099989796
First printing, May 1996

FOR MY SISTER LORRIE

ILLUSTRATIONS

The illustrations by artist Mary Newell DePalma, shown at the beginning of each chapter, represent important artifacts of early North American archaeology.

HOUSE OF MIRRORS Mimbres bowl featuring an armadillo with a deer mask

EMOTIONAL BAGGAGE Mammoth, once common in North America

CLOVISIA THE BEAUTIFUL Clovis (stone point) from New Mexico, fluted at the base to set easily into a spear

WOMEN'S WORK Hopewellian clay figurine of mother and child

COUNTDOWN Mat creaser used to crush fibers for making tule rush mats

BRIGHT LIGHTS, BIG CITY Mask, possibly used for religious and ceremonial purposes, with antlers carved in imitation of a deer

FIRST CONTACT Distinctive Nueva Cadiz beads, Spanish products from the sixteenth century

A GOOD WISH Prayer feather

IN OUR GRANDMOTHER'S HOUSE Broken Mimbres bowl

EAGLE'S NEST Anasazi mug

CONTENTS

ACKNOWLEDGMENTS

I WOULD LIKE TO THANK ALL THE PEOPLE WHO allowed themselves to be interviewed and/or quoted. In order of appearance that includes Bruce Trigger, Patty Jo Watson, Margaret Conkey, Joan Gero, Louis Redmond, Richard Begay, Ben Rhodd, Vance Haynes, James Adovasio, Tom Dillehay, David Whitley, Paul Martin, Don Grayson, Joanne Dickenson, Glen Doran, Bruce Smith, Dale Croes, Allen Johnson, Timothy Earle, Todd Bostwick, Brad Lepper, Lynda Norene Shaffer, Steve Lekson, Rochelle Marrinan, Rolena Adorno, Kathleen Deagan, Roger Echo-Hawk, Larry Zimmerman, Larry Benallie, Davina TwoBears, Roger Anyon, Lynn Teague, Catherine Cameron, Allen Funkhouser, and Kim Malville.

A number of people helped with background information. Douglas Bamforth at the University of Colorado was very gracious with his time. Jim Miller at the State

Historic Preservation Office in Florida was also helpful. Robert Peterson gave me a wonderful tour of the Hopewell Culture National Historical Park. Kathleen Henderson and Mark Hackworth of Northland Research filled me in on some aspects of contract archaeology. Anthony Klesert at the Navajo Nation Archaeology Department had some insightful comments. Bob Schiowitz at the Gila National Forest squired me around the 1994 Southwest Symposium. Steve Reneau of the Los Alamos National Laboratory shared some important concerns. Tom Shields from East Carolina University generously corresponded concerning Cabeza de Vaca. Andrew Gulliford from Mulfreesboro State University and Margaret Kimball Brown at Cahokia sent some good information.

I am also indebted to the staff at the Society for American Archaeology and the Crow Canyon Archaeological Center.

In truth, it is impossible to list all the people and authors who contributed to this project. I am grateful to every one, named and unnamed.

Some of this book was published earlier in a revised form, parts of "Clovisia the Beautiful" in *The Missouri Review,* "House of Mirrors" in *Southwestern American Literature,* and "Eagle's Nest" in *The Rocky Mountain News.*

A note on dates. Most of the dates here are radiocarbon ages. These do change when calibrated with tree-ring chronology. Dates before 5500 B.C. are outside this calibration range.

Finally, I would like to thank my editor, Sharon Broll, for her good cheer and energy, as well as my agent,

Felicia Eth. My husband, Peter, and my two children, Maria and David, are a constant support. Polly Walker was a great companion in the Midwest. My sister Lorrie Epling was the same in the Southwest and the Northwest.

CHRONOLOGY OF CULTURES AND SELECTED SITES IN NORTH AMERICA

CARBON 14 DATE	CLIMATE	ARCTIC–SUB ARCTIC	NORTHWEST COAST	CALIFORNIA	SOUTHWEST
1500				CANALINO	
	PACIFIC				
1200					*Mesa Verde*
	NEO-ATLANTIC	THULE		HOTCHKISS	*Chaco*
		BIRNIRK	GULF OF		
	SCANDIC	PUNUK	GEORGIA		*Pueblo Grande*
		IPIUTAK	MARPOLE		MOGOLLON I
AD 1					HOHOKAM
					ANASAZI
		NORTON	LOCARNO		
500 BC	SUB-ATLANTIC		BEACH		
		DORSET	*Hoko River*	BERKELEY	
1000					
1500					
2000		ARCTIC SMALL	EAYAM		
		TOOL		WINDMILLER	
2500	SUB-BOREAL				
				CAMPBELL	
3000		NORTHERN			COCHISE
		ARCHAIC			
3500		OCEAN BAY			
4000					
					BAJADA
5000	warm, dry				
	ATLANTIC			ENCINITAS	JAY
6000	ALTITHERMAL				
7000					
				SAN DIEGUITO	
8000	cold, wet	PALEO-ARCTIC		PLUVIAL LAKES	
	BOREAL				FOLSOM
9000					*Blackwater Draw*
	cold, dry	NENANA			CLOVIS
10,000	PRE-BOREAL			CLOVIS	
	(LATE GLACIAL)				
10,500					
11,000					

PLAINS	MIDWEST-SOUTHEAST	NORTHEAST	ELSEWHERE IN THE WORLD	
			Aztec civilization	
			Marco Polo in Asia	
	MISSISSIPPIAN		Crusades	
VILLAGE	*Cahokia*	LATE WOODLAND	Toltec civilization A.D.	1000
			Charlemagne	
		POINT PENINSULA	Black Plague	500
			Dark Ages begin	
			London founded	
			Birth of Christ	AD 1
WOODLAND	HOPEWELL	MIDDLE WOODLAND	Punic Wars	
	Newark Earthworks		Buddah born	500 BC
	ADENA		Rome founded	
	GLACIAL KAME	EARLY WOODLAND	Peking founded	1000
		ORIENT	Moses receives Ten Commandments	
	Poverty Point		Upanishad tradition in India	1500
		TERMINAL ARCHAIC		
			Stonehenge center of worship	2000
			Indus civilization in India	
			First libraries in Egypt .	2500
	OLD COPPER	LAURENTIAN	Mother Goddess in Sumeria	
			& elsewhere	3000
		LATE ARCHAIC	First and Second Dynasties	
			in Egypt	3500
			Rise of Babylon	
			Sumerian writing on clay	4000
		MIDDLE ARCHAIC		5000
				6000
	Windover			7000
	KIRK	EARLY ARCHAIC		
PLANO	DALTON			8000
		LATE PALEO		
FOLSOM				9000
CLOVIS	CLOVIS	CLOVIS		10,000
				10,500
				11,000
				12,000
		Meadowcroft		
			Cave paintings in Europe	13,000
				14,000

HOUSE OF MIRRORS

ON A SPRING AFTERNOON, UNDER A BLUE SKY, in a cold wind, my husband and I take a family picnic. Perhaps we visit Massacre Peak, south of our home in southwestern New Mexico, where the petroglyphs are hidden in a rough tumble of pink fractured rock. On the floor of an alcove we can see the round holes, a foot deep. A thousand years ago women sat here to grind seed and admire the view of distant hills. Nearby a masked man has been pecked into a secret shelf of granite. From a lonely boulder my husband gives a shout. He stands before a macaw, a scarlet macaw among the scrubby creosote, gray mesquite, and devilish cholla.

Perhaps we go to Old Town instead, a village full of people in A.D. 800. This is another wonderful view of the Mimbres River winding through a green lace of cottonwood trees. Where the ledge drops off, we check the eagle's nest, abandoned now and cluttered with debris. The village is a set of mounds pocked by illegal shoveling. Potsherds litter the ground like the jagged remains of a jigsaw puzzle, a million pieces, and none of them match. In the last few years archaeologists have returned to Old Town, and their orange survey flags flap incongruously, attracting butterflies.

If we have friends or relatives visiting, we will drive to our main tourist attraction, the Gila Cliff Dwellings National Monument in the heart of the Gila National Forest and Gila Wilderness. As we walk up to the cliff dwelling, I watch for piñon pines. It's a good year; the trees are full of nuts. The forty-room ruin looks like a doll's house set cunningly against the bluff. My six-year-old son peers into tiny cubicles with stone bins of tiny corn cobs. Another larger room carries, faintly, the whiff of decay. In the late thirteenth century a small band of farmers built this high home and lived in it for a generation. Then they left, like so many Americans.

My son is not impressed. Often enough on these trips, he and his older sister are bored. They prefer the playground at McDonald's or the aisles of Wal-Mart. They are drawn to more modern artifacts: baseball cards, Barbie clothes, fluorescent colors, flashing lights, shrill sounds, a miniature green plastic garbage can stocked with inedible red candy—only fifty-nine cents! How can a corn cob compete?

Like most parents, we impose our passion.

We explore a nameless site in the Gila National Forest. The pottery sherd I find is small, an inch square, its white background crossed by impossibly thin black lines. This color scheme dates it to the Classic Period of the Mimbreno Indians, a time of cultural renaissance, when artists produced painted bowls that are world famous today. Mimbres designs are unique, startling, complex, humorous, mythic, bold, geometric, bawdy—a man with a penis that has a little face, a little face sticking out its tongue. This sherd may have once been such a pot, with its interior picture of a crane spearing fish or a creature half-bighorn, half-snake.

"Look," I tell my daughter. "The woman who made this lived right here. Maybe she had a little girl. They sat here together, making pots."

I motion to the surrounding scrub oak and juniper trees, the grass and dirt and rocks that would not have looked so different eight hundred years ago. Before I leave I will put this sherd back exactly in the place where I found it. To archaeologists, artifacts are mainly important in context. Taken from a site, they become casual souvenirs and lose much of their value. I doubt that this little bit of clay will ever really be of scientific interest. But there is a truth in the habit of returning it so carefully. It belongs here with the scrub oak and juniper, the grama grass and mule deer, in context. I will put it back, certainly, after I hold it a bit longer.

I am thrilled. I am thrilled nearly every time I see in the dirt the simplest piece of Mogollon plainware, the corrugated surface of a cooking bowl, the glamorous black on white of a Mimbres pot. This is the treasure-seeker's glory. I found it. I found the Easter egg.

I do not know what links me to the person who shaped this clay. I cannot really imagine a specific woman; I tell that story only to my children. But I do feel a connection. This making of pots is part of what it means to be a human being. Perhaps it is the essence. Suddenly my own life seems like a dream. Wal-Mart, surely, is nothing but an amazing, amusing, fantastical dream. In the middle of that store, in a restaurant, at a street corner, I have often paused, confounded by an atavistic awe. Wow! I think, looking at a traffic light. Magic! Who did this? What happened to the world? Where are the trees? I am both appalled and appreciative.

Holding my sherd, I feel the substance of time, a place I can travel to while standing still. I heft its weight. This moment is a thousand years ago and a thousand years ago is this moment and we are both the same, that woman then and this woman now. Time folds in. I am at the center. It may be the closest I ever come to understanding quantum theory.

I do not feel this in museums. There someone else has found the Easter egg. My connection to this woman is directly linked to being outside. She lived right here. The sun is hot on the back of my neck. I smell pine needles and the faint current of rotting leaves. My heart beats its pulse of blood and, like her, I am just another animal in the landscape. I know the treachery of gravel slopes, the fear of starvation. Quickly I look around. If need be, my children can survive on piñon nuts. The trees are full this year.

Moving on, I search the ground for another piece of white-painted clay, perhaps for a stone flaked sharp enough to cut through muscle. The grip of this knife would not be strange. For 99 percent of human development, we fed directly from the earth. We craved the sweetness of berries for their ascorbic acid. We chewed the last bit of fat in the bison's hump. When we were cold, we tore open bears, ate their insides, and wore their outsides. We rooted up tubers and made medicine from trees. We imprinted on wilderness. We still carry this life.

I hold a stone worked by some ancient toolmaker, and I feel oddly patriotic. Over 200,000 years ago Homo sapiens began with a female hominid in Africa. (That's one theory, at least, and I choose to believe it.) My part of that woman migrated to Europe and crossed the ocean as soon as she could build a boat. She conquered the indigenous people mainly through disease, fished in New England, farmed in the Midwest, ranched in Texas, mined in Arizona, and sank into the ground with the persistence of a root seeking water. I love this country. I have sailed often over its breadth and width, by plane and car, marveling and adoring. The map of the Southwest is the map of my childhood. My backbone is the Rocky Mountains. I love this land. I cannot say it more simply or less emotionally. Its history is a history I need to know.

I am aware of irony. I carry the burden of those who declare love for a land their forebears took from other people. I will accept that burden, and still, I will not put down my love.

I love this country even as I mourn it. When the Mimbrenos lived here a thousand years ago, the Mimbres River was deep, fast, full of trout. Bighorn sheep clattered in the mountains. Wolves played tag in the grama grass. The land was young—and so lovely. Much of my interest in archaeology comes from the image it offers of a healthy America—clean air, clear water, abundant wildlife. This is my definition of wealth.

In the rural county where I live, there are three proposed Superfund sites, places where the poisons of abandoned mines have turned the streams eerie colors of blue and orange. Concentrates of lead blow from the tailings that resemble hills. By my house the Mimbres River is often shockingly dry, its water spent on alfalfa and apples. Giardia makes the stream undrinkable. The rangeland that rises above the valley like two brown wings has been overgrazed for a hundred years. The tall grass is gone; the arroyos are deepening. Everywhere I look I see diminishment and degradation, as do we all.

Archaeology, of course, is not really the story of a pristine environment but of humanity's impact on the environment. A thousand years ago the world of the Mimbrenos was neither young nor virginal. Their ancestors had known quite a different landscape, full of wooly mammoths, giant sloths, and tiny horses. Some archaeologists think it was the Clovis hunter, combined with a changing climate, who helped harry these animals into extinction. Later the Mimbrenos themselves would be forced to leave this valley as their population grew and resources declined. The Apaches came next, the Spanish, the Mexicans, the Americans, always conquering and being conquered, always feeding from the land.

Archaeology is the tale of our first awkward relationship, the wrestling match of humans with the natural world. It is a tale of peopling that in North America extends our cultural perspective back at least 12,000 years. The little room of the twentieth century opens onto a continent full of questions. Who were those men and women? How are we similar? Who are we?

So I go to the Gila Cliff Dwellings. I spend a Sunday at Old Town. I gather nuts from a piñon pine. As I walk, I search the ground for black on white, some jigsaw piece of a larger pattern. Stopping, I feel the sun on the back of my neck.

"Maria," I call to my daughter.

There is a macaw in the creosote, a masked face.

WE BEGIN WITH HISTORY. Archaeology is the study of the past. The practice of archaeology is a reflection of the present.

In *A History of Archaeological Thought* Bruce Trigger wields this idea like a knife. Nineteenth-century archaeology served mainly "to denigrate the native societies that European colonists were seeking to dominate or replace." The archaeological record revealed Native Americans to be vicious, primitive, and inferior. This made it easier to take their land. Social Darwinism helped. In the advance of human evolution, Indians were living fossils, incapable of progress, doomed to pass from this world.

By the early 1900s anthropology had developed more progressive ideas of culture, and archaeology had developed better field methods. Artifacts were busily sorted, pottery sherds typed, and populations schematized. Slowly the map of ancient America was being drawn.

Still, if overtly racist views were abandoned, certain stereotypes remained. "New ideas," Bruce Trigger writes, "such as pottery, burial mounds, metal working, and agriculture were almost always assigned an East Asian or Mesoamerican origin." American Indians were imitative, not creative.

During the Depression public-funded archaeology increased. After World War II the field flourished, energized by such discoveries as radiocarbon dating. Some archaeologists stopped labeling artifacts long enough to look at them. They began to explore social behavior, settlement patterns, ecology. A few questioned the very nature of what they were doing. In 1948 W. W. Taylor blasted his colleagues for their limited goals and lazy fieldwork. In 1953 Albert Spaulding complained, "Truth is to be determined by some sort of polling of archaeologists, productivity is doing whatever other archaeologists do, and the only purpose of archaeology is to make archaeologists happy."

It wasn't a bad description. It may not even be a bad thing. In any event, truth of a sort was on its way.

Bruce Trigger sets the scene: "The two decades following World War II were an era of unrivalled economic prosperity and unchallenged political hegemony for the United States. Despite the threat of nuclear war, this was a time of great optimism and self-confidence for most middle-class Americans . . . this self-confidence encouraged a relatively materialist outlook and a readiness to believe both that there was a pattern to human history and that technological progress was the key to human betterment."

In the 1960s, in the spirit of that decade, New Archaeology was seen as a revolution. A charismatic Lewis Binford argued that archaeology must and could seek the underlying rules that govern culture. He promoted ethnoarchaeology, the study of living people for analogies to the past. He viewed cultures as adaptive, problem-solving systems that evolved in predictable ways. He emphasized technology and the environment as factors in social change; he de-emphasized human volition or psychology. On a practical level New Archaeologists demanded a better sampling of sites and a more rigorous scientific method.

New, or processual, archaeology is described as positivist, which literally means that "knowledge is based on natural phenomena." The word also implies an upbeat, can-do attitude. Positively, science can answer our questions and solve our problems! More positively, archaeology can look at material remains and decipher the past.

For Bruce Trigger, New Archaeology followed other social sciences in its desire to produce "objective generalizations that could be used to manage modern societies." Without missing a beat, the author adds that archaeology married science just after the National Science Foundation emerged as a major source of funding.

By paying real attention to Native American cultures, New Archaeology helped end a century of racism. At the same time, processual archaeology ignored specific tribal beliefs, particularly in the area of religion. In the scientific equation of cultural change, people's beliefs had a small part to play.

In these heyday years Patty Jo Watson was one young professor who jumped on the bandwagon and began leading the parade. In 1971 she cowrote the popular *Explanation in Archaeology: An Explicitly Scientific Approach.* Over twenty years later she calmly lists the criticisms since leveled at New Archaeology.

"One—the philosophy of science had been oversimplified or misinterpreted. Two—not enough attention was paid to how a living community becomes an archaeological site, a process that can seriously obscure the past. Three—no attention was paid to the cultural *meanings* of artifacts. New Archaeology dehumanized the past and ignored ideology. Four—all causes for change or development through time were sought and found in eco-utilitarian or environmental mechanisms like population increase or climate change. Five—the research and results of New Archaeologists were shaped by their own social and political prejudices. Worse, they hadn't noticed."

Today New Archaeologists are the old guard. As Bruce Trigger says laconically, "a growing number of archaeologists are prepared to believe they can never achieve an objective historical understanding of the past."

Bruce Trigger's own work is grounded in honest subjective bias. His history of archaeology portrays a white middle class struggling to keep and justify its power base. Later, as that power base eroded, New Archaeology's "denial of a creative role for human beings" reflected "the dehumanizing effects of the growth of corporate capitalism." This Marxist view is an important truth. Archaeology reflects political economy.

But truth is no longer a prize that can be found by polling. Archaeologists are too eclectic. In a field that some describe as confused, postprocessualism includes many different ideas and approaches. Most archaeologists still pursue a basic timeline. Some seek larger cultural patterns. A few look for the mind of early man—and early woman. In this house of mirrors there are multiple ways of knowing the past.

FEMINISTS MIGHT BEGIN with the anthropologist Claude Lévi-Strauss and his observation of natives in South America, "The entire village left the next day, in about thirty canoes, leaving us alone with the women and children in the abandoned houses."

Wait. What did he say? The extraordinary invisibility of women has resulted in assumptions like very big rocks, hard to turn over.

Margaret Conkey, a professor at the University of California at Berkeley, says, "Archaeology is consistently told to us from a male perspective that adopts 'male' as the norm and proceeds from the male experience." Basketry, seed collecting, shell fishing, and plant gathering have been undervalued and underresearched because they are "women's work." The female's experience is assumed to be the same as the male's. A hunting and gathering society is egalitarian if the relationships between men are equal. In fact, males and females may be treated very differently.

In a paper called "Genderlithics," Joan Gero pushes against one big rock called Man the Toolmaker. Most archaeologists still agree that flint knapping was a male activity. This is important, since toolmaking is tied to our very identity as a species. Moreover, the better our tools, the more advanced or civilized we are. Joan Gero points out the obvious. Paleolithic women, who made up half the population and did half the work, constantly needed tools for basic chores such as butchering meat, scraping hides, cutting plant material, and hunting small game. "It is inconceivable," she exclaims on the page, "that they sat and waited for a flake to be produced, or that they set out each time to borrow one." Common sense tells us that women must have been creating tools all the time, every day. Living cultures tell us the same thing. In North America, Lewis and Clark reported seeing "squaws chipping flakes into small arrow points."

Toolmaking is male because archaeologists focus on a narrow range of tools used for hunting and warfare. Joan Gero believes that archaeologists don't even see or classify quickly made, unretouched flake tools. They don't see women making beautiful, elaborate, retouched tools because tools and tool boxes, hammers and saws, power drills and staple guns belong to the modern Western male.

Archaeology deals with the origins of humanity and its biases are uniquely powerful. We validate the present by finding it in the past.

Margaret Conkey objects to the very way archaeological papers are written, with "their cults of authority: the authority of statistics, of the passive voice, the exaggeratedly objective eye, the single line of evidence, the single cause, the only perspective." She believes that a feminist archaeology means more than "add women and stir." An archaeology that engenders the past tries to see men, women, and children interacting with each other and with their environment. Clearly the houses are not abandoned when the men leave, and when we understand better what is happening in these houses, our ideas of the past may radically change.

"An archaeology that takes gender as a valid, central, and important concept," Margaret Conkey says, "parallels an archaeology that foregrounds the individual as an active social agent."

Margaret Conkey would focus on the people of ancient history, not the remains. For Native Americans this is just a beginning. They insist that archaeology deal with living people as well. This shift in perspective—and in the balance of power—is the most significant change in American archaeology today. It has been driven by new laws that give Native Americans the right to reclaim their sacred artifacts and skeletal remains. In 1990 the Native American Graves Protection and Repatriation Act

(NAGPRA) mandated the return of these items from national museums and institutions to the appropriate tribes. It gave recognized tribes control over unmarked native graves and sacred areas on public land. State laws often complement federal ones. Old and new skeletal collections are now being reburied. Certain forms of excavation and research are now being protested—and denied.

At a 1994 conference, a panel of Native American archaeologists faced an audience of their Anglo colleagues.

"If we don't evolve," Louis Redmond, an Iroquois from the Nebraska National Forest, suggested, "then archaeologists will find themselves in court more and more for desecrating sites. We won't be able to pay our lawyer bills! Archaeologists are going to have to go to Indian people and define relevant research questions that will benefit Indian people. When I ask my elders how I can do archaeology, they say, 'Show me how it will benefit the seventh generation to come, and we will allow it.' These elders are not interested in answering some esoteric academic question. They are interested in that seventh generation to come."

"We have to change our very language," Louis said. "That term prehistory. To my uncle, prehistory was the time of the dinosaurs. Archaeology is still using some very prejudicial words."

"You have to go back to the people," Richard Begay from the Navajo Department of Archaeology confirmed. "You have to go back to the tribal government and to the local people. You have to work with them from the beginning."

"Archaeologists do not go out and have a sense of relationship with the land." Ben Rhodd, a Potawatomi, scolded. "When you view landscape as a sense of home, not as a riverine system, then you will begin to understand what we mean by sacred places. When two tribes meet, we begin first to talk about the land and then we are actually talking about the people. When I walk out as a Native American, I know my grandparents have seen this land and my great-grandparents. When we say sacred, we mean the entire landscape, not some little part of it! These sacred places are not a commodity. You can't own them. You can only be a guardian."

"Still," Ben Rhodd relented later, "white archaeologists can magnify things out of proportion. All it sometimes takes is sitting down with the people you fear and talking with them on a human level. A lot of it is your approach as an individual."

For archaeologists, sitting down with people on a human level is new. The pace of working with tribal governments is new. The loss of their unquestioned right to dig up and analyze artifacts is new. Some archaeologists see only loss. Others recognize that this is anthropology, their chosen profession, the meeting of world views. Forced into contact, these views vibrate with tension. They do not, necessarily, implode. Science as culture. The landscape as culture. The seventh generation to come. This is personal, professional growth.

A popular question now pervades American archaeology: who owns the past? Native Americans, archaeologists, landowners, museum curators, and collectors look into the mirror. Each has an answer.

Meanwhile, whoever literally owns the past can make a lot of money. In 1990 a Southwestern polychrome pot sold for $250,000; a Mississippi ax went for $150,000; a prize arrowhead brought $20,000. Everywhere, sites are being bulldozed legally and illegally. Mounds are torn apart. Petroglyphs are chipped from rock walls.

In the valley where I live, Mimbres sites have become a windfall, like finding oil in the ground. The Mimbrenos often put burials under the floors of their homes, "killing" painted bowls with a ritual hole before laying them over the faces of the dead. Landowners must now contact an archaeologist when they uncover these remains. The human bones are reburied. But without a proven link between the Mimbrenos and any modern tribe, the funereal artifacts can be kept and sold. A nicely decorated pot might bring in $25,000. A neighbor of mine once found seventy-two in her front yard. That kind of math inspires people.

Patty Jo Watson describes American archaeology as "one gigantic conservation and salvage operation." She looks to a time when all the sites are gone, all the sacred places desecrated. "Soon we will have only excavation reports and museum specimens," she warns, "a tiny fraction of the record, fractions of fractions of the past."

Besides looting, development and construction—highways, suburbs, shopping malls—are rapidly paving over the traces of the last 12,000 years. Again, new laws have given archaeology a new mandate, cultural resource management, the oversight of a disappearing heritage.

On the panel of Native American archaeologists, Louis Redmond was trying to get his sobered audience to laugh. He fiddled with the buttons on his high-tech microphone. A red light flashed. The sound blared on and off. "I'm fascinated with the stuff on this podium," Louis confided. "I guess I have that trinket-bauble thing."

Next, he held up a cartoon in which one Native American proclaimed, "The white man took everything. They left us nothing, nothing, nothing!" The other Indian chirruped, "What about our glorious sun tans?"

These jokes carry a sting. "You've been here five hundred years," Louis told us. "You haven't been wasting your time."

"Okay, let's have some questions," Ben Rhodd coaxed.

"What about when *we* are caught between two tribes?" someone finally asked, "I work with the Navajo and with the Hopi . . . and, you know . . ."

Louis Redmond grinned at Richard Begay, who stood up and paused for a long time. "I'll need a moment here," Richard explained, "to produce the appropriate politically correct response."

Now the archaeologists did laugh.

"That's good," Ben Rhodd exclaimed. "We want you to do that. You have to have some levity. You have to have some joy."

JOYFUL THINGS are happening in archaeology.

I like to imagine a middle-aged woman. She is not exactly in a midlife crisis. But she *is* in a ferment of change. There are dangers ahead, opportunities, crossroads. Now she has the distance to analyze her childhood, the experience to evaluate her future. She knows herself to be rather complicated.

Long ago she looked for meaning. She is prepared to look again. She ranges from angst (the past is inaccessible, all versions of the past have the same value) to arrogance (only archaeology can show us the breadth of human experience, when the land was young, young and so lovely). She is at some point of maturation. There is a great deal to think about, and she would love to think and ponder all day.

Instead, she has to go to work, pick up children, pay bills, visit friends, and make a dentist appointment. Practical demands take up her time, even as insight burns in a sliver of glory. I like to imagine archaeology as a middle-aged woman, harried, healthy, stopping for a minute in the grocery store with an important thought on the nature of the universe. Blinded, she pauses in the cereal section. Distracted, she picks out the corn flakes.

It is no coincidence that this woman resembles me.

EMOTIONAL BAGGAGE

I AM SITTING IN GOOFY'S KITCHEN IN CALIFOR-
nia's Disneyland Hotel watching a tall skinny Goofy (or is
that Pluto?) give a round young woman a terrifying hug.
The woman does not respond warmly, but her friends at
the table hoot in delight. Like many people in this room,
they are archaeologists who came here to attend the annual five-day Society for American Archaeology (SAA)
conference. This year the meeting has attracted 2,000
members, with over 100 symposiums and 500 papers
read.

Why the Disneyland Hotel? I have no idea. But I
love the juxtaposition. I feel sure there is an epiphany

here, something about how far we've come in the last twelve thousand years, served on a bed of bafflement as to what exactly we've come to. I can see the teacups, those big blue and pink saucers swirling around and around; I can hear the music—it's a small world after all; and part of me is already on the silver monorail that leaves the hotel every twenty minutes like a bullet straight to the heart of Disneyland. The Pirates of the Caribbean lurch and leer. Sleeping Beauty wakes with a start. Consumerism has never been so innocent. I applaud the humor of the SAA. There is an epiphany here, although I haven't found it yet.

Privately most archaeologists agree that conferences like these can be boring. A typical symposium involves a half-dozen speakers. One by one, each gets up to read aloud a written, scholarly paper. These are the kind of people, by and large, who skipped oral interpretation in high school. In any case, the delivery of something called "Computer Simulation of a Diachronic Model Portraying Village Adaptive Behavior under Environmental Stress" can only be jazzed up so far. Of course there are always some surprises and the occasional revelation. Academic feuds are also entertaining, but the insults are subtle, for insiders only.

What will really happen at the Disneyland Hotel is what happens whenever you confine a large group of people: social frenzy. This is the time to see old friends, to find a job, to find jobs for your students, to find some funding, to lament your lack of funding, to talk about your dreams, to evaluate your marriage, to reassess your appearance, and to discuss your research over one more beer, one more glass of wine, one more whiskey.

About the annual SAA conference, archaeologists speak with pride and horror. "It's a zoo!" "It's a circus!" "It's crazy!" "Oh, you really see those cocktail party eyes," Patty Jo Watson says. "While they're talking to you, people are always looking around for someone more important they should be talking to."

Situations like these bring out my inner adolescent. I hate parties. No one likes me. Get a grip, I tell myself as I walk through the vivacious crowd. Writers are outsiders. You are here to do an interview.

Specifically I want to talk about first settlement—when and how and who first entered the New World. For over a hundred years the question of when has dominated an aggressive and sometimes slanderous debate. In geologic terms the Pleistocene was a series of ice ages that ended, by our count, 10,000 years ago. A variety of megafauna probably went extinct at the same time. We now live in the Holocene, a very different world. The arrival of humans from across the Bering Strait during the Pleistocene meant a great deal to some archaeologists in the nineteenth and early twentieth century. They believed, passionately, that people had been here for a very long time. A later arrival—after 10,000 years ago—meant as much to others.

In 1932 the discovery of stone points near the bones of a mammoth in Clovis, New Mexico, confirmed that early Americans had been hunting Pleistocene mammals.

These Clovis people used distinctive large spear points, fluted at the base to fit into the split end of a wooden shaft. Vance Haynes has determined that Clovis tribes lived in the Southwest from 9200 to 8900 B.C.—or 11,200 to 10,900 B.P., "Before Present," the preferred academic form. Similar points, as well as variations, were soon found across the country, coast to coast, north to south.

With Clovis as a model, archaeologists agreed on how they would identify ancient sites. Vance Haynes intones, "The primary requirement is a human skeleton or artifacts that are clearly the work of humans. Next, this evidence must lie in situ within undisturbed geological deposits. The artifacts should be directly associated with stratigraphy. Finally, the minimum age of the site must be determined by a direct link with fossils of known age or with material that has been reliably dated."

People had been living in New Mexico 11,000 years ago. After 1932 archaeologists greedily expected to find even older sites. They didn't. Or rather they did, again and again, only to have each one disproved.

Vance Haynes had a premonition in 1959, when he and a friend explored a Paleo-Indian treasure chest in a gravel deposit of chert and quartzite. "The more we looked, the more artifacts we found, and the more we found, the greater our excitement," Vance remembers. They believed, youthfully, that they were looking at some pretty old stuff! Later they realized that all their scrapers and knives and tools had been chipped naturally while being carried along nearby streambeds. In the uplands cruder "tools" were the product of trampling animal hooves.

"The experience alerted me as to how often natural processes produce objects mistaken for the work of humans," Vance says. For such mischief, he coined the term "geofact."

In 1962 Vance was asked to investigate the Tule Springs site near Las Vegas, Nevada. The excavation boasted hearths carbon-dated to 28,000 years B.P., along with horse, bison, camel, and mammoth bones apparently butchered and cracked for their marrow. On closer look the charcoal hearths were really deposits of incompletely fossilized plants. The bones, again, had been broken by animals.

Three years later the National Geographic Society funded Vance and others to evaluate the Calico site in California, where human artifacts thought to be 200,000 years old had been found. Promoted by Louis Leakey, the site's tools were being picked from hundreds of thousands of chipped stones that occurred naturally in an alluvial fan. Vance Haynes suggested that, in the millions of pieces excavated, the artifacts were "statistical flukes of nature." Today few archaeologists support Calico's claim of early hominids.

In 1973 *Science* magazine trumpeted the radiocarbon dating of a 27,000-year-old bone tool in the northern Yukon. "If I have learned one thing in a quarter century of direct involvement in radiocarbon dating," Vance says, "it is that radiocarbon dates can be wrong." Such dates require an organic sample with carbon 14 isotopes. Vance suspected that the part of the caribou bone used for dating had been contaminated by older carbonates in groundwater. Unfortunately most of the bone flesher was destroyed to obtain the 27,000-year-old number. Within a decade, however, the development of accelerator mass spectography (AMS) allowed scientists to use very small samples of carbon. In 1983, 0.3 grams of the flesher was extracted and dated at A.D. 600.

In 1975 an article in *World Archaeology* declared that human bones and skulls, again from California, were 70,000, 40,000, and 26,000 years old. The excitement was based on a technique called amino acid racemization (AAR), which measures the rate at which amino acids change chemically after an organism's death. AAR must be calibrated with radiocarbon dates from the area. In this case the scientists used a skull which they thought was 17,000 years old. When AMS dating pushed that down to 5,000, the other bones fell like dominoes. Another spectacular announcement was spectacularly wrong.

By the early 1990s the Clovis date had become the Clovis barrier. Clovis-Firsters held the conservative, mainstream position. Pre-Clovis enthusiasts kept finding new sites. Imagine Calypso music and a long wild party brawling until dawn; 11,000 B.P. (9000 B.C.) is the stick these party-goers are trying to "limbo" under.

For some archaeologists that image is too benign. David Whitley specializes in rock art. "Ron Dorn and I were dating petroglyphs, and we had the misfortune to obtain pre-Clovis dates. We tried to publish our data, as good scientists, only to see vitriol and scorn heaped on us and our newly developed techniques. I became involved in the topic because I was so annoyed with what I viewed as the unprofessional attacks on our work."

David Whitley believes that Clovis-Firsters wrested "political control of the debate. They controlled publication reviews and were able to influence what was said and where. This strangled discussion by not allowing the opposing view, pre-Clovis, to be argued in the mainstream literature. . . . it was a kind of cognitive apartheid. It hindered the quality and quantity of pre-Clovis research, but it also hindered the development of the Clovis-First hypothesis. If no questioning of doctrine is allowed, doctrine tends to get sloppy."

In 1993 David and Ron published an article showing that with a migration rate of four miles a year (once suggested by Vance Haynes), leaving New Mexico in 11,200 B.P., Clovis people could not have reached those sites in South America that Clovis-Firsters had already approved. David grumps, "That was the first full-length article supporting pre-Clovis that *American Antiquity* has published in at least two decades.

"The issue is the oldest and most acrimonious in the profession. I suppose I am really in this for the challenge," he admits. "As the youngest of four siblings, how can I resist?"

Many archaeologists (it is hard to say how many) think now that the Clovis barrier has been smashed. That dance is done.

Two sites in the New World stand out.

The Meadowcroft Rockshelter, a small overhang in southwestern Pennsylvania, has been used by humans since Paleo-Indian times. Symbolically, the site was abandoned by Native Americans during the American War for Independence. The deposits here include the earliest corn in the area (375–340 B.C.) and the earliest squash and ceramics (1115–865 B.C.). The late Archaic (4000–1500 B.C.) shows an increase in the use of the rockshelter. The middle and early Archaic (8500–4000 B.C.) highlight the industrious processing of deer, elk, bird eggs, mussels, hackberries, nuts, and other fruits and seeds. Deeper down, the Paleo-Indian tools are surprisingly sophisticated. One point looks like an ancestral form of Clovis.

James Adovasio and his team began excavating this site in 1973. Material from each stratum was sent to four different laboratories for dating. All but four of the fifty-two radiocarbon dates are in chronological order, dutifully following the stratigraphy. The out-of-order dates are minor flip-flops in the later periods. The earliest six dates, from a stratum associated with unquestionable artifacts, range from 14,000 to 10,800 B.C. The average of these—12,000 B.C., or 14,000 years ago—is James Adovasio's estimate for the first humans at Meadowcroft.

Not everyone agrees. The plant remains from the site's lowest level are black gum, oak, and hickory. Animal bones include white-tailed deer, southern flying squirrel, and passenger pigeon. These are not ice age species. Yet at that time Meadowcroft was a hundred miles from the glacial front.

Always courteous, always professional, Vance Haynes suggests that once again the radiocarbon dates may be wrong. Perhaps this material has been contaminated by older carbonates in the groundwater, or by nearby coal, or by ancient wood thrown into Paleo-Indian firepits. He would like to have an AMS date on one of those early plant samples.

James Adovasio believes that the low-lying, south-facing Meadowcroft Rockshelter was in a microclimate, common in the complex mosaic of the late Pleistocene. He notes that four different labs found no sign of coal contamination, that the water table has always been below the lowest occupation level, that there is no coal seam within one-half mile of the rockshelter, and that the use of ancient wood would not have provided such consistent dates. He says he has nothing left to date and no reason to do it.

At the Disneyland Hotel James and I sit in a cheerfully bright and tasteful lounge. James Adovasio is an intense man. Like others embroiled in the long question of when, he is a little weary. At times over the years, he has been angry and defensive. Today these emotions are washed to the palest residue in a smile. In the background Snow White holds the arm of a boy whose mother quickly takes a picture. The mother is pleased. The little boy looks stunned.

"The excavation at Meadowcroft was state of the art," James Adovasio tells me. "We had enormous amounts of money and resources. The techniques we used had spinoffs in a hundred different applications—we are using one now to help catch pot hunters across the country. We had a wonderful interdisciplinary team. The point of the enterprise was the enterprise itself. In retrospect I shouldn't have let the issue of those early dates cloud the methodological aspects of the project.

"I took classes from Vance Haynes years ago, you know, and I share his critical perspective. My views are not radically different from his in terms of the evidence I want from a site. At this point virtually everything he has asked us to do we have done. For me, now, the information at Meadowcroft is incontrovertible that humans were living in that rockshelter between 13,900 and 14,500 B.P. It's a closed issue. If it's still an open issue for other people, there's nothing I can do about it. I am not interested anymore in trying to convince everybody.

"It's a curious thing. I work a lot with perishable items, with basketry and textiles. If I were to go in front of a group of archaeologists and say that Archaic people in the Ukraine were weaving, oh, nets out of larks' tongues, they would go, Huh! Hum! Larks' tongues! But they wouldn't disagree. There would be no uproar. Our emotional involvement with the first Americans is so great that any detail is tremendously questioned. The earliest, the first, always charges us. That kind of baggage can make the trip harder."

I ask James Adovasio if the trip has been too hard or, at least, too emotional.

"There are a lot of emotional aspects in any scientific discussion," he agrees. "There is always acrimony when people stake out intellectual positions they believe are integral to their reputations and careers. Sometimes the questioning has tipped over into a theater of the absurd. . . . But, no, I think the process has generally been fair and necessary. Acute scrutiny will continue, and it should continue."

In that spirit James Adovasio, Tom Dillehay, and others recently went to South America to investigate the Pedra Furada site, with its bed of 40,000-year-old charcoal hearths. "We were not impressed," James says now.

Tom Dillehay is the archaeologist who excavated Monte Verde in Chile, the second site believed to have pre-Clovis dates. Most Paleo-Indian camps appear to be a collection of stone tools. But at Monte Verde, peat and a high water table kept organic remains miraculously preserved. Here archaeologists can see what is left of twelve rectangular huts with log foundations and a pole framework draped in animal skins. Near a wishbone-shaped structure was a cache of salt, mastodon remains, and chewed boldo leaves—a medicinal tea still used by indigenous people. The recovered items at Monte Verde include wooden mortars, worked bone, ivory tools, and a human footprint in clay. The deposits containing this material are all in perfect stratigraphic order. An average of thirty radiocarbon dates place this site at 12,800 B.P., almost 2,000 years before Clovis.

Five feet down and 250 feet away, in a sandy level with poor preservation, the research team also found three hearths containing charcoal, with stone items of which three are clearly artifacts. This charcoal dates to more than 33,000 B.P.—and *this* number makes the research team nervous.

Concerning the oldest level, James Adovasio and I have a curious exchange. "Yes," he says, "that material looks empirically good. It looks good to me. But 33,000 B.P.? It's a matter of making that intellectual leap."

"But as a scientist," I wonder, "if the evidence looks good, aren't you supposed to make the leap?"

"Well, that's how the process is alleged to work."

"Is the long history of this debate causing a cautiousness . . ."

"Oh, there's no question!"

". . . that might be too cautious?"

James Adovasio pauses. "Uh. Maybe. We are working in areas where the frontiers are being pushed. Maybe I am overcautious. But I've seen so many of these older sites fail. Fieldwork is not the same as a laboratory experiment."

Later I will have the same conversation with Tom Dillehay. Tom, too, is convinced that his dates on the upper site are sound: people were at Monte Verde 12,800 years ago. The proof for this has become "overkill, over-analysis, overdone." But as for that older level . . . 33,000 years ago. . . .

"It follows the four criteria. We have an intact geologic record, almost a pancake sequence. We have artifacts which are in a tight geologic context. The radiocarbon dates are good. In this case, in the geologic deposits, we have Latin America's best work, over a hundred dates in the same kind of stratigraphy. Technically speaking, as an archaeologist, I cannot reject that kind of empirical evidence. But as the interpreter of the site? As Tom Dillehay? I don't accept it intellectually."

As Sharman Russell, a child of this century, I have a great attachment to the word empirical. I believe in my fourth grade vision of science. I believe in scientists holding the string of a red balloon, flying through the clouds, into outer space. So I insist. "But aren't you *supposed* to go where the evidence takes you?"

"No," Tom says decisively. "For that upper level, my intellectual thought and my empirical data have a strong marriage. For that lower level, they are strongly divorced.

"If I were to accept that date," he continues, "I'd have to explain it within the peopling of all the Americas. Given the present archaeology in Russia and Siberia, I just don't see people being here 25 to 30,000 years ago. I can see 20,000. I can see 17 or 18,000. But that lower level . . . I'm not being shy or a coward. It just really bothers me. We have no affinities between that lower site and the upper site or between it and any site anywhere."

"But *empirically* . . ." I'm stuck on that word.

"Right. I've gone through all the possibilities. So far I can't find anything to make me believe it is empirically wrong. I have colleagues who tell me the data is obvious. It doesn't make certain people happy when I say I can't commit myself. But for me, that deeper level . . . is unresolved."

I want to shout: fly through the air, Tom! In this, of course, I am being naive. Tom Dillehay and James Adovasio are quite right in their commitment to irresolution. Only fools rush in where archaeologists fear to tread.

"Archaeologists destroy the evidence as we excavate it," Tom reminds me. "A site excavated is a site gone. At that point the only thing we have to rely on is everybody's interpretation, maps, photos, artifacts. We have to completely trust the investigator's procedures and process. We can't replicate or redo our work. Also, this early Paleo-Indian material involves such a particularly ephemeral, inconspicuous archeological record. It's very difficult to deal with."

Fieldwork is not a laboratory experiment. Even laboratory experiments can be misinterpreted. David Whitley says that excavation is inherently destructive. Some people compare archaeology to interviewing an informant and then shooting him.

Ambiguity remains the truer science. Mystery is central. First settlement reads like a whodunit with an aggravating number of suspects, plot twists, wild cards, and missing evidence. Diverse fields outside archaeology have brought new insights—and as many controversies. Linguists track migration through language. Physical anthropologists study the evolution of teeth. Molecular biologists look at genetic human markers. The research is exciting. More often than not, it is also contradictory.

We are not even sure if humans came here from northern China via the Bering Strait (as Tom Dillehay assumes). Perhaps they paddled along the northwest coast or floated across the Atlantic Ocean. Asians could have reached North America in a few distinct migrations or dribbled over like a melting ice cream cone from all different directions. New finds in Florida may have dates at 12,000 B.P.; one archaeologist suggests these people came from Spain.

"Extraterrestrial transport?" I joke with Tom Dillehay.

He pretends to think. "I'm unresolved on that."

A middle-ground theory might go like this: a band of Mongoloids split from a northern Chinese population after 21,000 B.P. They left traces in eastern Siberia around 20,000 B.P., in eastern North America by 14,000 B.P., and in Chile by 12,800 B.P. They may have come in three major migrations that can be linked to three modern populations: the Na-Dene, the Eskimo-Aleuts, and the Amerinds. Around 11,000 B.P. the population grew to the point that people became visible in the archaeological record.

Or not. This could be partially, mostly, or completely wrong. In a rare consensus archaeologists agree on one thing: the peopling of the New World will be solved when the New World is peopled by more archaeologists. What keeps the game hot is that any new site, at any time, could explode under our noses. It might be in your backyard right now, in the next housing project, the next state highway, the next dam, the next quarry pit. In fact, such sites are exploding all the time like little firecrackers. A Russian archaeologist claims to have found artifacts from a stratum in Siberia more than two million years old. In southern New Mexico, Richard MacNeish believes he has human hand prints in clay dating to 28,000 B.P. Rumors from Florida continue to circulate. Then there is South America: Pedra Furada, Taima-Taima, that lower level in Monte Verde.

Tom Dillehay, for one, is relieved to get his head above the fray. Before Monte Verde he studied complex societies. He's glad to return to the Incas of Peru. Wryly he notes that people at this conference have been friendlier to him. It's not the influence of Minnie Mouse. It's an academic turn of the tide. Monte Verde has been pivotal, and even harsh critics now ask the right kinds of questions. There is a sense of applause. Tom Dillehay has limboed with flair, right under the Clovis barrier.

Mischievously he pretends not to notice. Did I just walk under something? His 1994 final report, published fifteen years after the excavation, was blandly titled "Monte Verde: A Late Pleistocene Settlement in Chile, the Archaeological Context."

"I completely avoided the issue of first settlement." Tom grins. "I'm not that intellectually interested in it— although I understand we have to have chronology to line things up. In this case the debate has taken us away from other important issues. What happens when modern Homo sapiens undertake a long distance trek through territory that has never been occupied? That only happened here in this hemisphere. We should be looking at things like dispersal and migration. I define Monte Verde as a site that represents people on the move. If some archaeologists are disappointed that I haven't put out a big neon light flashing pre-Clovis, pre-Clovis, then that's their problem."

BEFORE I LEAVE the Disneyland Hotel, I talk again with David Whitley. As we stroll past the hotel pool, we stop while a glass carriage crosses our path. A livery man in gold and silver, with whiskers and the nose of a rat, drives the carriage pulled by two ribboned horses. Inside, a girl sits dressed in a ballroom gown. I gape.

David lives a few hours from Anaheim. "Someone's getting married," he observes.

"People do that at the Disneyland Hotel?" I try to imagine starting marriage dressed as Cinderella.

David nods without judgement.

Like many in his field, David decided to be an archaeologist when he was young, younger perhaps than most, "about two years old, a dumb time to make a major career choice." At twelve he saw the cave paintings of France. "Beautiful. Fascinating. That hooked me on rock art. Unfortunately, I was too naive to know it was a taboo subject."

Rock art research, like first settlement, is challenging and controversial. Unlike first settlement, rock art has been marginalized in American archaeology, mainly because most petroglyphs and pictographs cannot be dated.

Could not be dated. In David's *American Antiquity* article, he presented six California petroglyphs and surface artifacts that ranged from 12,000 to 26,500 B.P. Simply put, he peeked under the rock varnish, a coating of minerals and oxides that form on exposed rocks in dry areas. Organic matter such as algae and lichens, growing after the petroglyph or tool has been made, can be trapped between the rock and this varnish. An AMS date of the organic matter gives a minimum age for the artifact.

Suddenly, David Whitley is talking about microstratigraphy, the way a Holocene layer of rock varnish, poor in manganese, lies on top of a late Pleistocene layer of rock varnish, rich in manganese. This excavation digs up electrons. The trowel is elephantine.

Vance Haynes, to be sure, has his doubts. Many critics question the techniques used in rock varnish dating. They worry that ancient dust could contaminate the material under the varnish. Importantly, these researchers have been unable to duplicate the lab work done by David's partner Ron Dorn.

David Whitley proselytizes, "Rock art dating opens up new categories of data, categories that have been ignored." He hopes to look into the minds of those who first came to the New World. From the study of living tribes, we know that rock art is often linked to shamanism—the magic of menstruation or rain or a good hunt. David talks about entoptic images, neuropsychological patterns that form "behind the eye" when hallucinogens are ingested. Eight entoptic patterns are found in rock art across cultures and continents. David believes that geometric patterns in the Coso Range of California were part of someone's vision quest 19,000 years ago.

In Goofy's Kitchen again he confides, "I see the growth of archaeological knowledge, taken at a disciplinary or a personal level, as a process best described in narrative form—a story with heroes and villains, plots and subplots, texts and subtexts."

This statement gives me the courage to complain: archaeologists have reduced first settlement to a feud about dates. But this is a powerful, wonderful, biblical, numinous story. Was it lonely crossing the Bering Strait?

What did that woman think as she sat on a hill and nursed her child? Did she understand that every thought she had—about this plant or that animal—was a first thought? Surely she smelled something new and extraordinary. What was this intoxication, this fear, this impact of being human in a nonhuman world?

Why don't archaeologists talk about these things?

David admits with some embarrassment, "As a group, well, archaeologists are best characterized as anal retentive and pathologically oriented towards the concrete and mundane. Why else would anyone spend their lives sorting pot sherds? Even me, I'm not sure there are any people in my view of the peopling of the New World."

Ironically, it is the skeptical, conservative Vance Haynes who dares to speculate at the end of an otherwise demure paper: "In any case, I hypothesize that, sometime between 13,000 and 12,000 B.P., an adventuresome band, perhaps still looking for megafauna, moved southward through an ever-widening corridor between the waning glaciers in search of game. There may, however, have been another motive. Exploration could have been just as powerful a driving force 13,000 years ago as it was in 1492. As long as there was forage, a charismatic leader, bent on seeing what was over the next mountain or around the next bend, could lead a band of like-minded individuals who would find the ice-free corridor an intriguing and challenging place, perhaps leading to happier hunting grounds. Once away from other bands, there would always be the lingering question of, 'Who is ahead of us?' Sooner or later they would suspect that maybe no one was ahead. This would be an awesome realization."

It's not just being first. It's being only. Tom Dillehay said it in his own way: we should be studying migration and dispersal, people on the move. We should be studying that giddy and frightening smell of newness, the impact of being human in a nonhuman world, the meaning of loneliness.

There is an epiphany here, if we can only find it.

CLOVISIA THE BEAUTIFUL

VIOLENCE WAS ON MY MIND WHEN I WENT TO see Paul Martin at the University of Arizona's Desert Lab in Tucson. The night before—my first night in town—I had stopped at a convenience store to make a phone call. A teenage boy grabbed my purse. We scuffled, he ran, and I was on the ground, my wallet still gripped under my arm, my legs waving feebly. I felt like an overturned potato bug. For minutes afterward my throat hurt from the shock of my screams. That is what impressed me most, my own primitive sound, an instant familiarity with adrenaline. Back in the car, my hands were clenched with power. Crime, of course, is on the rise in

Tucson—drive-by shootings, gang graffiti, theft. Paul's wife has been attacked in her own kitchen. All this, suddenly and absurdly, seemed like a big surprise.

Paul Martin is a well-respected scientist with three degrees in zoology and over forty years of teaching and research experience. A large man, he uses a cane, sometimes two, when he walks, having been tempered by polio in the 1950s. His perspective on social violence is unique. Sheltered in his office, we talk of nineteenth-century Masai warriors who at the age of fifteen were "unstoppable, with the ancient need to prove to themselves and their families that they could risk and be challenged." We discuss the long evolutionary history of human beings, the crucible of hunting and gathering, the utter wildness of children—and of Paul's vision in which children at the close of the Pleistocene killed off the slow-moving, bear-sized Shasta ground sloth, a creature that lived where Tucson gangs battle now. Possibly these children speared the sloth for sport and target practice. Possibly they helped cause its extinction 10,000 to 12,000 years ago.

Like Paul, I have come to believe we have not made our peace with the Pleistocene, this grand chunk of time which lasted nearly 2 million years and included over twenty ice ages when glaciers advanced and retreated. Ten thousand years ago the last Pleistocene ice age was over, and 73 percent of the large mammal genera in this country were gone. (Genera is the plural of genus, between the family and species.) We know that eight genera died with the Shasta ground sloth: the mammoth, mastodon, giant short-faced bear, camel, horse, tapir, short-legged llama, and saber-toothed cat. Presumably another twenty-six genera went extinct in North America at the same time. To fully understand the loss of two-thirds of our large terrestrial mammals, you must first imagine—think of it as remembering—a land where cheetahs, lions, capybaras, four-horned antelope, giant peccaries, brush oxen, pampatheres, and dholes exist beside the species we know today. Life was measured on a different scale. Beavers weighed 300 pounds. The Florida sloth loomed as big as an elephant, and glyptodonts with armored tails and turtle-backed carapaces cruised slowly by, early versions of the Volkswagen Beetle.

The disappearance of these mammals is unexplained and may always be so. The end of the last Pleistocene ice age meant that most of North America became hotter, and the extinctions are reasonably linked to climate change.

In the 1960s, however, Paul Martin looked at the fossil record and had a revelation. Many more big mammals, especially those over 100 pounds, had died off than small ones. Also, although extinctions are a natural phenomenon, these were unusually large in number and seemed to occur very rapidly. None of this matched the pattern of extinctions before, during, or after earlier ice ages. Animals like the horse, camel, mammoth, and mastodon had survived here for millions of years through a multitude of climate changes. Why would they wait for the end of the Pleistocene to die?

Paul Martin is a Clovis-Firster. For him (and others), the oldest evidence of human beings in North America still dates to about 11,000 years ago. These big-game hunters appeared on the scene at the same time America's "big game" started to go extinct. This may not be a coincidence. In Paul's overkill, or blitzkrieg, theory, the hunters who came out of Siberia faced animals who had never known nor feared the human predator. Spears, in particular, must have been a novelty. Suddenly the claw of a lion, the bite of a tiger, could come in the wind. Suddenly, without warning, there was a stone in one's heart.

With an unlimited food supply and little human disease, Paul's hunters multiplied at a rate of 3 percent annually as they moved south and east, about ten miles each year. In a matter of centuries they would have reached the tip of South America. Even when only a third of them are killed, slow-breeding mammals often cannot reproduce fast enough to survive overhunting. Computer models show that humans could have eliminated the continent's megafauna in a wavelike front that left behind zones of extinction.

With the decline of prey, carnivores such as the saber-toothed tiger and lion also disappeared, as did scavengers like carrion-eating storks and teratorns. Most of the animals that remained were smaller and more gracile, able to run fast or hide in wooded cover. Most, like the bison, had Old World ancestry; their genetic "knowledge" of European hunters may have given them the necessary edge.

New overkill models put people in America for as long as 20,000 years before human population overwhelmed the megafauna. Overkill does not depend on the Clovis-First thesis, although "Blitzkrieg goes to hell," Paul Martin admits.

For thirty years he and his friends have expanded overkill into a model that explains extinctions worldwide. Global overkill begins in Australia where 86 percent of mammals died off after 30,000 B.P. In North and South America massive extinctions coincided with the appearance of Clovis hunters 11,000 years ago. Yet at this time Africa and Eurasia had relatively few losses, presumably because animals there evolved with human predation. Much later, from A.D. 1 to 1000, human colonists arrived at isolated islands like Hawaii, Madagascar, and New Zealand. Here, mega and minifauna would also vanish within a few centuries. In Hawaii over fifty land bird species were eliminated by the first Polynesian settlers.

For overkillers the extinction of large tasty mammals clearly does not track climate. As far as we know, climate changes at the end of the Pleistocene had no effect on animal populations in the sea or on islands. They had relatively little effect in Africa and Eurasia. Instead, like a dark shadow, extinction follows the footsteps of humanity. Unstoppable, wild, from the cradle of Africa, we spread over the earth.

At this point any good director would crank up the music. The murderer advances. Lights flicker uncertainly over the marsupial lion, the ground sloth, the mastodon, the glyptodont, the elephant bird, the pygmy hippo, the flightless moa. One by one, the victims fall.

PAUL MARTIN might object to this analogy. The overkill theory is not really a film noir, and Paul Martin is not really a gloomy guy. In fact, he is having a great deal of fun. He remembers his first ground sloth dung with tender enthusiasm. Frozen by aridity in the American West, such dung is a small and gentle miracle.

"I sat down in this cave in the Grand Canyon," Paul says, "and I could feel the hairs rise on the back of my neck. I was sitting on the shit of Shasta ground sloths. And it was so *fresh*. It wasn't hot and steaming. But it didn't look very old either. I could see the rest of our field party coming up toward the cave, below me, in the cool of a February morning. And at that distance, I had to think of early hunters. Then the hairs on my neck really stood up! It was an emotional experience, an emotional charge. You can't go into one of these places and not feel the spiritual power. I was sitting on the dunghill of an animal that no longer exists and that no one knows. I was time-traveling . . ."

Paul radiates the happiness of a man whose work and pleasure are the same thing. "At times like this, there's a wonderful feeling that *this* isn't the real world," he confides. "This isn't the world I'm locked into. It's as though I'm suspended suddenly above the ground, no gravity! and I'm sweeping around and around through the last thousands of years."

Later Paul dated the dung of Shasta ground sloths from seven caves throughout the West. As he proudly points out, dung is "rich in uncontaminated organic carbon, in convincing association with an extinct animal, perfectly ideal for radiocarbon dating." The youngest material, sawed off from the tops of the piles, was 11,000 years old. The abundance and ages of the other samples pointed to a quick demise of the sloth, not a slow, patchy decline.

In this case, Paul argues, it is hard to blame climate. Dung is a lovely source of dietary information. These Arizona sloths mostly ate globe mallow, with a bit of Mormon tea, prickly pear cactus, saltbush, or yucca. In some places the desert ecosystem where they lived lingered for thousands of years after they disappeared. The Grand Canyon caves also yielded the bones, horns, and dung of the extinct Harrington goat. Again, a healthy population of goats left the area at the same time as the Shasta ground sloth. Things may have literally gotten too hot for the boreal goat. But sloths have a tropical ancestry. The odds should have been in their favor.

"We don't prove things," Paul cautions. "What scientists do is test various best guesses or, to be blunt, bedtime stories that might explain the mystery."

Paul's bedtime story includes slow-moving, perhaps bad-tasting ground sloths that were "so easy to dispatch even children could use them for target practice. Generations passed. With time, the more desirable game became scarce. Eventually the Garden of Eden was stripped of its mammoths, mastodons, sloths, and dozens of other species. The surviving game was restricted to a few large animals that were more resistant—that is, less huntable. Like the hunters, most of these had Asian relatives. With the extinctions, human populations crashed and the few survivors broke into isolated, smaller, more warlike tribes."

For nearly 10,000 years people would live in balance with the species who had survived that first onslaught. Not for the first time, and not for the last, we had changed the shape of the natural world.

THE OVERKILL THEORY can be convincing. In popular literature and science, it has had a long life. Still, the majority of archaeologists disagreed with Paul Martin in 1967 and continue to disagree with him today. Among professionals overkill is the underdog. At the same time, the model is possessed of such pizzazz that for twenty-five years it has forced its opponents to (1) spend time and energy poking holes in it and (2) come up with better ideas of their own.

Don Grayson is such an opponent. In 1976 he sent a paper to Paul on bird extinctions in North America. Don argued that the loss of nineteen genera of North American birds at the end of the Pleistocene could not be explained by overkill. Paul countered that many of these birds had been dependent on the extinct mammals.

"I told him he had a great subject," Paul says fondly, "and the worst possible answer. He acknowledged me in the footnotes and made none of the changes I told him to make and that's the way it's been ever since."

As he talks, Paul often uses the terminology of fencing. "I'll make the first cut," he might begin in a friendly voice. Don Grayson is one of his favorite partners.

Don has many objections to blitzkrieg.

If people hunted horses, camels, sloths, and tapirs, we should have "kill sites" that associate the bones of these animals with human weapons. But the only proof we have of Clovis big-game hunting is a few dozen spearpoints with a dozen mammoths and maybe a mastodon.

Don questions the belief that all thirty-six genera of mammals went extinct at the same time. We know that nine genera disappeared quickly between 10,000 and 12,000 years ago. We don't know that the others did not die off earlier or more gradually.

He scoffs at Australia, where the chronology of settlement and extinction is so unclear it can be made to fit either the climate or overkill theory. Some paleontologists point to a drought after 26,000 B.P. that lasted millennia. Meanwhile, the time for human arrival keeps getting pushed back, perhaps as far back as 60,000 years.

Don shrugs at Madagascar. Yes, people on islands caused extinctions. But island ecology is unique. Islands and continents are apples and bananas.

Most importantly, Don Grayson is pleased to announce that better climate models *are* being developed. Average annual temperatures rose at the end of the last ice age. But if arctic air masses were no longer blocked by the ice sheets of Canada, winters in central North America actually became colder (and summers hotter). Seasonal differences in temperature were more extreme. Ecosystems became less complex and could no longer support the diversity of Pleistocene fauna.

While small mammals did not go extinct at this time, they were affected. The yellow-cheeked vole now lives in the Arctic; it once ranged as far south as Tennessee. The collared lemming also retreated to Alaska. With their faster reproductive rates, small creatures could adapt. Big lugs like the Jefferson ground sloth could not.

Other critics doubt Paul's description of a hunting-and-gathering society. Hunters and gatherers do not grow as fast as 3 percent annually, nor do they expand through new territories at ten miles a year. Hunters and gatherers are a cautious, conservative, low-fertility type; they do not blitzkrieg.

For those interested in ping-pong, overkill enthusiasts refute:

We haven't found many kill sites because it happened so fast—in less than five hundred years. Statistically we are lucky to find any kill sites at all.

Only Don Grayson won't "make the jump" that thirty-six genera disappeared in a pulse of extinction. Don is being difficult.

Okay. Australia is weak. "But it is strikingly like America in one respect," Paul Martin says. "Kill sites and the butchering of extinct animals are very hard to find in its fossil record. Again, this suggests a quick wipeout of the extinct fauna."

Anyway, we still have a better global model than you do.

Those new climate theories? They are the stuff of good science. Keep working.

But small mammals! Pleeease. Small mammals are always moving around. Were these changes unique to the late Pleistocene? Even if they were, the important question remains: why did big mammals die off at the end of *this* ice age and not during earlier climate changes?

Point. Counterpoint. Follow the white ball. This game, I guarantee, will last into the night.

AT MY TUCSON HOTEL I wake to the color of red lights flashing. A twenty-nine-year-old man has spent the night here with a thirteen-year-old girl. When I go down to get coffee, the girl's mother is on the phone, angry, frantic, speaking in Spanish. The East Indian hotel manager is also frantic, for different reasons. I am still processing my wrestling match with the teenager who pushed me to the ground. Vividly, my body remembers the event, a sharp rock under my shoulder, the sound of screams. I had clutched my wallet so fiercely! In a moment, on my back, I would have started kicking. The impression that remains is one of wordlessness—pure fear, pure anger, nothing to remind me of who I am.

Later I remembered how the boy had been watching me, and I knew my body had sensed the future. Later I began to make up stories. Unhappy with the image of myself on the ground, I scrambled up and ran after my attacker until he too fell to the earth, amazed to find a forty-year-old woman in pursuit. I did not want to hurt him. But I wanted to prevail. (In real life, I run five miles three times a week, quite slowly, pleasantly.) In other stories, the boy holds a knife. He aims a gun. I know how lucky I have been.

In front of my motel the lights of the police car confirm a worldview of perpetual danger. The hotel manager hovers near the woman now weeping on the phone. I leave for another appointment with Paul. This time I will also meet Don Grayson who has come to lecture on Pleistocene extinctions at the University of Arizona. In my mind the scuffle over a wallet, the pain in this mother's voice, and the deaths of animals thousands of years ago are all becoming oddly, illogically, ineluctably intertwined.

Don and Paul stand in front of the Desert Lab examining cactus pads chewed on by nearby, free-ranging javelinas. These men are good friends. According to Don, their friendship "arose from the fact that we disagree so thoroughly on the Pleistocene extinctions." This is not the academic norm. Paul Martin, in particular, has a long career tied to the defense of overkill. His friendship with Don Grayson is another small and gentle miracle.

Clearly such a relationship requires technique. Don and Paul keep their disagreement constantly in sight, poking it, bouncing it, throwing it up in the air. A good joke is a score. When Paul gives the introduction to Don's lecture, he concludes with a sigh, "Get it *right* this time, Don." When Don shows the illustration of a dour-faced glyptodont, he ad-libs cheerily, "Looks a bit like Paul, doesn't it?"

In his midforties, bearded, bright-eyed, Don Grayson is gifted with youthful energy. His research subjects range from the Neanderthals to the Donner party. Quick and intellectually combative, as he leans forward with sudden interest, he does not dart—but the action is implied.

Some twenty years older, Paul Martin moves and talks more slowly. At some point in our conversation, after Don makes a particularly legalistic point, Paul shakes his heavy head. "Now that's the kind of incisive thrust that leaves me gasping. I'll wake up at night thinking about this. A wicked argument! Can you imagine being in court with this guy?"

What I imagine is Jimmy Stewart as the country-bumpkin lawyer, helpless before the silver-tongued city slicker. Helpless as a moray eel. Don is quick. Paul Martin is immovable.

Others have been impressed by Paul's resilience. Don complains in print that the 1967 overkill theory was "so powerfully framed" that "Henceforth, most scientists were to argue that either climate or people, but not both, provided the driving force behind the extinctions."

"The debate," Don writes, "has been enlivened by the exceptional skill and force of the partisans, but that very skill and force helped entrench the members of each camp and has made it less likely that a cherished hypothesis would be abandoned and more likely that a masterful piece of advocacy on one side would evoke an equally or more masterful statement on the other."

In Don's view the middle ground has been lost, the discussion polarized. "Of course, I think that's fine," Don tells me. "I don't prefer the middle ground myself."

Why not? I wonder. It's my favorite place.

So I ask Paul why he and Don won't move an inch to the more comfortable, synergistic position. Reasonably, climate change took some animals to the edge of a cliff, and humans pushed them over or vice versa. In the West, for example, a drought 11,000 years ago may have caused mammoths to congregate at watering holes which made them easier for Clovis hunters to kill. This was a two-punch, knockout, middle-ground blow.

"That's a terribly tempting thought," Paul says, "because so much of science is politics, and politics is compromise. But it's part of the temple vow of academics to drive plausible theories as far as possible—to see what they are made of. That's my mission. If I don't push overkill, we won't learn where it can go. I expect the same from the climate partisans."

"Exactly," Don agrees. "Even if Paul is wrong—which, of course, he is . . ." Don waits for Paul's laughter. "His model has a heuristic value. It's easy for people to understand how this could happen. We know the kind of impact we have on wildlife today. Paul's argument resonates intuitively. People didn't cause the Pleistocene extinctions in North America. But they still had a tremendous effect on the land, as did people in the Old World and everywhere else. It's a common mistake to think of Native Americans as benign, invisible presences, like butterflies or bunnies."

Don is right. More and more, research reveals an early America that was vigorously harvested, pruned, planted, irrigated, logged, fished, and hunted. Don mentions California's Sacramento Valley, which shows a long-term decrease over thousands of years in the abundance of large and small vertebrates. Paul talks about central Arizona in A.D. 1000, when the Hohokam were mostly eating mice, rats, and rabbits. In 1519 Cortez invaded Mexico, and the spread of European diseases like smallpox reduced native tribes by as much as 90 percent. Wildlife rebounded. By the 1700s Europeans saw a country that rattled their imaginative powers, a land swarming, teeming, erupting with animals. But this abundance was unusual, a blip on the screen of the last 10,000 years. The wilderness was more illusion than fact.

Paul shakes his finger at the environmental movement. "Ecologists see that deer eat grass and wolves eat deer and all this is part of a healthy ecosystem, the circle formed by predators and prey. But look at what is missing. Where is the human hunter and gatherer who has shaped this country for millennia?"

People, strangely, were left out of the circle.

That, Paul believes, has distorted our notion of what is natural—ecologically PC. We've been messing with creation ever since we were created. We can't stop now. What is natural anyway? Mammoths in the Southwest? Paul Martin gets excited. He dreams of introducing the elephant, perhaps the rhinoceros, to southern Arizona. After all, trampling proboscideans once dispersed the fruits of desert trees like the mesquite, an eco-niche we have elected to fill with cows.

Don Grayson is incredulous. "Do you mean . . ."

"I mean we shouldn't sell this country short," Paul insists, "by saying that nature intended us *not* to have mammoths here after 11,000 years ago!"

Don leans forward. "The rhinoceros . . ." he begins.

They are off. I am left holding the thread, a placental rope, that takes me back to the first human hunter. A normal extinction rate is one species per million a year. In the rainforest we have increased that a thousandfold. Bulldozers are a good symbol of our destructive power. Perhaps the spearpoint is another. This is not about overkill, right or wrong. This is about looking into a deep well. The reflection wavers. We lean dangerously over the edge. Who is down there? All parents know that children are capable of using ground sloths for target practice. We sense the intensity with which teenagers need to face death and give birth. We are a violent species in a violent world. Crisis-oriented, our memories are short, a single lifetime, a single generation. We have already forgotten that grizzly bears, jaguars, and wolves once roamed the Southwest. Against the grain, Paul Martin does not want us to forget the mastodon.

"If there's a better answer for the Pleistocene extinctions than human predation, that doesn't change the stakes," Paul says. "The loss of the mammoth is still tremendously important. This country is still being discovered and evaluated. We need more verses to "Home on the Range." We need to include the glyptodont and the giant beaver. We have the potential here for a New Patriotism, one that goes back ten thousand years! Clovisia the Beautiful! We should celebrate our deep history."

Some scientists suggest that recent world history also hinged on the loss of our Pleistocene mammals. New Worlders had a smaller pool of species to domesticate—no horse to revolutionize warfare, no beast of burden for agriculture, no pig or sheep as an additional food source. In Europe these animals encouraged an earlier population growth and rise of urban centers. Thus Columbus discovered America before Montezuma discovered Portugal. At the same time, domestication resulted in a plague of diseases that swept through and immunized the Old World. Once brought to America, these diseases were the real conquistadors.

Paul Martin complains that Clovis sites in Arizona and New Mexico are being neglected. He wants memorials and national monuments and a visiting politician. If this were a sports game, Paul would be wearing a Clovis hat and a Clovis T-shirt with a Clovis banner in one hand and a fat hot dog in the other. Clovisia the Beautiful.

That evening, as Paul drives me back from a local restaurant to my hotel, I sit cramped between him and Don in the front seat of a battered pick-up. When it is time to say good-bye, the door on Don's side will not open. Laboriously, Paul must get out of the driver's seat and go around the truck in order to release us. Paul walks slowly, using his cane. The night is surreal as spotlights from a crime-fighting helicopter flash into the next block. The night is electric, rich with speculation. I am still happy on a single beer. Don and I begin to clown around. "Out, out!" He beats at the recalcitrant door. "Let me out!" Paul takes his time.

"All right," I say. "We give up. It was people."

"People," Don picks up the cue. "People did it! Men, women, children. They killed everything. Just let us out."

"People did it!" We chorus.

Paul wrenches open the door. Don Grayson tumbles out.

"So," Paul grins. "You admit it now?"

Don dusts himself off with mock dignity. "No," he says. "I lied. It was climate."

UNDER A BLUE SKY at Blackwater Draw in Clovis, New Mexico, I feel at last on solid ground. Eleven thousand years ago this was a spring-fed lake, where we know Paleo-Indians camped and hunted. We have found their spearpoints in situ with mammoth and bison bones. We have found other bones as well: horses, camels, peccaries, ground sloths, an extinct antelope. We have uncovered a half-dozen turtles stacked on top of each other and cooked in their shells. We have grinding stones and knives glossy from cutting plants. We have picked up Clovis points placed in the lake's spring conduits; Vance Haynes believes they were meant as a prayer.

Blackwater Draw is the "type" site for the Clovis culture, one of a handful of Paleo-Indian sites open to the public. Unfortunately for many years it was also a gravel quarry, and most of its treasures have been crunched or carried away. Still, fifteen mammoth skeletons were excavated here, over half of these associated with Clovis points. The trail guide to the site begins dramatically:

"The time is 11,300 years ago. Imagine that you are enjoying the view of the lush vegetation on the Llano Estacado. The spring-fed Blackwater Draw is a favorite place to hunt. You remember how much better this water tastes than the last water hole. It feels good to rest for a moment, watching the insects and birds fly around. The group of hunters you are with suddenly become alert. A tense excitement is mounting as a loud awesome sound is heard. You recognize this as the sound of a mammoth. Wanting a drink of water, the animal is tromping through the tall grasses that surround the lake. Your extended family members have begun stalking toward the sound. They motion with hand signals for you to go in a certain direction. Everyone prepares for the flurry of action to come. The spear throwing stick is aimed and ready. The Clovis spear points are sharp. Hopefully one will pierce a vital organ and cause the huge creature to die. You check your weapon and prepare to throw. The signal is given and the attack proceeds. The mammoth falls. The band of hunters rush to finish the kill."

Obviously, killing mammoths is exciting. This is another fact. Archaeology is not *that* ambiguous. Trying to recapture a Pleistocene thrill, more than one researcher has spent his funds throwing Clovis spears at dead animals, watching African natives stalk game, butchering circus elephants, or flint knapping perfect fluted points. These men are clearly having fun. They've also learned that quartzite holds a better edge than chert, that the main effort lies in cutting through hide, and that the trunk is a portable source of fat. Some have watched elephants mired in ponds and wondered if Clovis hunters were not scavenging rather than hunting. Others feel sure this was *mano a mammoth,* a carefully selected animal isolated from the matriarchal herd, wounded, crippled, stalked, defeated.

In Paleolithic research mammoths are one icon. The Clovis spearpoint is another. Archaeologists have long been drawn to its phallic strength and beauty. Clovis hunters must have felt the same way, for they only used top-quality flint, even when that material was hard to get. The classic Clovis point averages nearly three inches, with parallel edges, a sharp tip, and two vertical "flutes" removed from each side of the base. Fluting thinned the bottom so that it required a smaller haft, and the flute scars served as a slot to seat the spear. Relatively hard to make, a fluted point is a form of technology. Some believe it was also a form of art or ritual or identity.

No one knows where fluting originated or why. Vance Haynes thinks it was "made in America," a technological response to the abundance of game or to environmental stress. Alternatively, fluting may have evolved in the Arctic out of a microblade tradition (small flint flakes inserted in wood or bone) or the lanceolate point. We don't know if the idea of fluting spread through existing populations or if fluting was carried physically by colonizing hunters, but variations of Clovis points have been found across the Americas. They provoke the startling, perhaps misleading image of a widespread, uniform Paleo-Indian culture.

"Oh, archaeologists just love points." Joanne Dickenson, director of Blackwater Draw, shrugs. "And the Clovis point is pretty. It's very pretty. But it's not the important thing. These people were mainly eating plants and roots and nuts and berries. They hunted, of course, when animals were around. But ethnographic studies show that hunters and gatherers in temperate areas get 70 percent of their diet from plant foods. I don't think these Clovis people were much different."

Many researchers now believe that Paleo-Indians are best described as complex foragers, not big-game hunters. Some archaeologists joke that Clovis tribes killed one or two mammoths in a generation and then never stopped talking about it. We do have kill sites, stone points, and animal bones. We also have techniques, for the first time, that can examine pollen and plant remains. The future of Clovis research lies in seed collecting. The focus is on diversity.

"Paleo-Indian research is opening up," Joanne says. "Clovis has become a shorthand for all Paleo-Indians in that time period. But clearly, people in different ecosystems lived differently. We are looking at new kinds of things."

Joanne, herself, is a new kind of archaeologist. A rancher's wife, mother of four children and grandmother of five, she started college when she was forty years old and got her M.A. nine years later. When we talk at Blackwater Draw, she talks about fourth-graders and high school students.

"We're trying to help teachers teach archaeology," she says. "Archaeology can involve so much—geology, math, botany, biology, soil science. It gives kids a concept of time. It deals with prejudice. It leads them all right back to themselves. It's a puzzle and a detective novel. It teaches logical thinking. Oh, you know, we've got to get these kids to think!"

This is a former PTA vice-president, a Girl Scout, Cub Scout, and 4-H leader who has shepherded one boy and three girls through the American public school system, 168 days a year, 12 years each. We talk about the future of Clovis, New Mexico. "The water table used to be visible at this site in the early sixties," Joanne says. "Then farmers started to irrigate heavily from the Ogalala aquifer. The water keeps dropping, and it's not going to come back up, not with the agriculture here and the new dairies. We've quadrupled the number of dairies in the last three years! They're coming in from California's San Joaquin Valley. They've depleted the water there, so they move here. But this area won't withstand massive development, not for long. When the water is gone, it's gone. We'll go back to desert and dunes and grassland."

Joanne worries about the cottonwoods that now shade the Blackwater Draw site. If the water table drops too far, they will be gone as well. So she's planting other grasses and scrub brush, drought-tolerant plants against the drought that's sure to come. Archaeology has extended her sense of time. The dairies will come and go, the cottonwoods will die, the sand dunes will grow tall as they did in the dust-bowl days her father lived through. Although she has deep roots in Clovis—her grandparents homesteaded nearby—she wonders if her grandchildren will be able to live here. She wonders about the seventh generation to come.

"There's a lesson at Blackwater if we'll only listen. These people lived from the land and so do we. We can't keep using things up the way we've been using them. We have to monitor what we're doing to the landscape because that's how we survive. Once we destroy where we are living, we think we can move on to somewhere else. But eventually there is nowhere else to move. We're going to end up like Africa or Asia.

"We have to become more simple. I think of my grandmother. She grew her own garden, her own meat, she canned every year. Of course I lived through the Russian era, the bomb shelters. My grandmother always said, 'I have three years' worth of food in the pantry. You all know where to come!' "

I lived through that era too, those old bomb-shelter days. They aren't really gone. Most Americans have a sense of the apocalypse, World War III, the end of Wal-Mart. Often enough archaeology reminds me not of how things were but of how they could be again. Often enough I have left an exhibit on flint knapping or basket weaving, and in my boredom is the guilty thought: you should have paid more attention. You may need that someday.

"We have to get more simple," Joanne repeats. She is quiet for a moment. Perhaps, like me, she is thinking that she should can this year.

I leave her office and begin the trail through Blackwater Draw. The site reminds me, frankly, of an abandoned gravel quarry. I read the guide, examine the geology, and try to picture that mammoth kill. An outside display shows the exposed bones of *Mammoth columbi* and *Bison antiquus* growing strangely from rock, impossible flowers. Layers of color map the stratigraphy of bedrock gravel, fluvial deposits, clay, diatomaceous earth, and carbonaceous silt. I learn that Folsom followed Clovis, Portales followed Folsom, and Archaic followed Portales. Early Americans used this place for 7,000 years. The names and dates soon blur. Other questions resonate. Were they different? Was it better?

To the first question, Joanne Dickenson says no, as do Vance Haynes and other Paleo-experts. Vance Haynes is here today mapping a well he thinks was dug by the Clovis people. "They had the same gray matter as you or me," he says. "They were at a different stage in their technology, that's all."

The second question is like hitting a bruise, the pain of our postindustrial angst. Was it better? In the last two centuries we have had small but diverse groups of hunters and gatherers to study. Some had lots of leisure time; some didn't. Some starved on occasion; some hardly ever. Much depended on the physical environment. Still, this doesn't touch the heart of the question, which is about spirit not matter. Was it better emotionally? Were we better? Were we more alive, more human, more engaged?

Anthropologist Robin Fox says yes. He mourns the "Paleoterrific" not because it was better but because it is where we belong. There we reached "the limits of our evolutionary adaptation." We were few in number, tribal, creative, dependent on nature, in awe, in touch, in our natural setting. We were home.

At Blackwater Draw I walk the trail, which is not long, circling the site three times. It is hot, dry, and windy. I'm glad I don't live here.

"I once asked an engineer," Robin Fox writes, "why cars were built to achieve speeds like 120 m.p.h. that they almost never attained and couldn't use except for brief periods. He explained that if you wanted a car to have a cruising speed of, say, 85 m.p.h., then it had to have a capacity of 120 m.p.h.—to maintain the 85. The problem is, with an ambitious driver, there is a temptation to want to cruise at higher and higher speeds. Could it be that the Paleolithic brain (which is our brain, it hasn't changed) was geared to cruise at the "paleoterrific" level, but in consequence had to be capable of the industrial and post-industrial societies? That what we have done is put our foot (as it were) ever more firmly on the cerebral gas pedal simply because we *could* go faster? And that now we are trying to cruise at what were only intended as passing or emergency speeds? We are doing 110 m.p.h. in a car designed for 85 because we can do 120. But, I asked the engineer, for how long? Not very long, he said. It's all relative, of course, but not for very long."

Was it better? We'll never know. We don't even know the meaning of better. We couldn't go back if we wanted to. Archaeology is not about nostalgia. Archaeology reminds us that what we are doing today, right now, is a tiny sliver of the human experience. We look at that other experience and at our own and we wonder: should we go to a movie tonight or a potluck? Is the endangered species act important? Is mass transit? Population control? Can we live more simply? Can we imagine fewer cars? Where will we move when we have used up this place?

These concerns belong to the future, not the past. Sometimes we are led to them via the Paleolithic, our deep history.

I think we miss the animals. We miss the glyptodont, the four-horned antelope, the gentle ground sloth, the 300-pound beaver, the wooly mammoth, and yes, the short-faced bear and saber-toothed tiger. We miss, literally, their weight and number. Our American West once rivaled the Serengeti Plain. We were surrounded, outnumbered, by otherness.

As I drive away from Clovis, New Mexico, I see a flat brown landscape under a large blue sky. Occasionally in the next eighty miles, a cow or two will be grazing in the distance. If I stop and look closely, I will find the snakes and lizards.

The fact is that I love to drive fast over long distances. I sail away from Blackwater Draw, listening to a Joan Baez song on the radio, singing loudly, loving this life. On one side of the highway are green fields, monotonous rows empty of everything but monotonous green plants violently sucking up the waters of the Ogalala. In fifty years that water will be gone. On the other side of the highway, quietly waiting, is the desert, sand and sage and sparse grass.

I think we miss the animals.

If I stop and look closely, if I stop and squint against the sun, still I won't see them.

WOMEN'S WORK

THEY LIVED NEAR THE COAST OF EASTERN
Florida between 7,000 and 8,000 years ago, or 5000 to
6000 B.C. Small game was plentiful. Plants, too, were important: hickory nuts, acorns, persimmon, elderberry,
grape, prickly pear, cherries, plums, and roots. From the
fiber of palmettos, they wove cloth. From stone, wood,
and bone, they made tools. Children often died young,
but adults frequently lived into their seventies. People
took care of each other. When one older woman injured
her shoulder and arm, a relative or friend nursed her until
she was well. A boy had crippling spina bifada; the tribe
provided for him until his death from infection at the age

of fifteen. Arthritis plagued them, as did gum disease. Still, on the whole, these were a people who ate well, loved well, lived well.

When someone died, he or she was wrapped in cloth and buried with things we call artifacts. A bone awl and a shark's tooth. An atlatl hook. A bottle gourd. No one, seemingly, was buried with more pomp and circumstance than anyone else—except for the children who were given a little more care, a few more grave goods.

When someone died, he or she was taken quickly to a nearby marsh, placed in a grave of muck, and pinned there by long sharpened stakes. The mineralized water was only slightly acidic. The wet peat prevented further decay. Seven thousand years later the bodies in this ancient cemetery are remarkably preserved. Many of them still have brain tissue sheltered in the skull's curve, the brain shrunken to one-fourth its normal size, the wrinkled hemispheres shockingly visible. From the cortex of these, molecular biologists are able to extract mitochondrial DNA—the codex of lineage.

This Florida collection of skeletal remains is one of the oldest and largest and most demographically complete in North America. The Windover site was discovered in 1982, when a backhoe operator noticed bones in the black peat he was dredging from a pond. At the landowner's expense two samples were dated to over 5000 B.C. From 1984–87 Glen Doran from Florida State University helped excavate the site. It wasn't easy. To dewater the pond 160 well points had to be driven into the ground, pumping 700 gallons per minute, 24 hours a day for the first several months. Eventually two-thirds of the burial area, containing 169 bodies, was removed before the land was returned to its original condition.

Today residents of the Windover housing development bicycle and jog on the narrow road that runs past the pond and sandy hammock. Saw grasses cut the air. Herons glide discreetly. Oak, pine, and cabbage palmetto fill the interstices between houses. A motor starts up. A boy's voice rises and falls and stops abruptly. This is a quiet suburb, with its own secret dramas.

Glen Doran will spend the rest of his professional life thinking about the meaning of Windover.

"Our models of hunters and gatherers are probably overstated in terms of harshness," he says. "The image is that people were always on the edge. But that doesn't seem to be the case here. These were sophisticated folk in terms of their wood and bone tools. They were well-adapted to a rich ecological area. They had leisure time for activities like weaving clothes, bags, mats. Definitely, the category of material that stunned people the most was the fabrics. We knew there had to be basketry and textiles at this time period. But all we had were tantalizing hints. You could have held the entire collection of early Archaic textiles in your hands. When we started seeing these large body coverings, I was frankly skeptical. The excavator came over, and she said, 'You know, the peat is coming off in a strange way.' The photographer said, 'Oh, it's fabric, it's fabric.' And gradually it became clear—this was fabric! In a case like this, you bail out. That afternoon I contacted James Adovasio, one of a handful of experts in the world, and he came down immediately. He was here within a few days, going from burial to burial, shaking his head. He was amazed. We were all sweating a lot, thinking about how to preserve these things that were just a shadow of what they had once been, like something woven out of wet spaghetti. If we had let it dry, we'd have cigarette ash."

Glen gives me an enthusiastic, detailed description of how peaty, saturated fabric can be conserved through a technique developed by Union Carbide. These days his concerns center around conservation and analysis. The Windover bones are in demand. Archaeologists want to compare them with other collections. Doctors want to compare them with modern skeletons to get "time depth" on problems like arthritis and lower back pain. At the mention of lower back pain, I remember to sit up straight. Glen Doran, a physical anthropologist, also shifts his position. Back pain affects over 80 million Americans. Is it the price of walking upright? Or the result of lounge chairs? The Windover bones could help answer these questions.

All this brings up a different issue.

"Reburial, yes," Glen says. "It's never far from my mind."

The 1990 Native American Graves Protection and Repatriation Act mandated all federally-funded institutions to inventory their collections of human remains, burial goods, and sacred artifacts—and to inform the appropriate tribes. Tribes who prove a cultural affiliation can ask for the material back. To some extent museums

benefited from the process. "We learned a lot about curation," Glen Doran says. "We went into those dusty storage rooms and discovered what was there." The result in
paperwork was staggering. Some tribes received thousands of letters from museums across the country. Glen
Doran says wryly, "Native Americans are being faced
with a whole other burial issue."

NAGPRA meant the return of many ancient remains with their associated goods. Most traditional Native Americans believe like Cecil Antone, a Pima, that
"No living man on earth has the power to infringe on an
individual who has been laid to rest or to keep his or her
bones stored in a box for eternity." For Cecil Antone, to
be stored in a box is an unnatural act, a form of imprison-
ment. Some Native Americans fear that to disturb human
bones is to disturb the larger harmony of the land and of
the modern tribe itself.

Florida, however, is unusual. By 1763 the entire indigenous population had died off from disease and warfare; that year, the Spanish took away the last surviving
Timucuans. Later, Seminoles and Miccusukees moved
into the state, where they live on reservations today.
Gene studies show that the Windover population is unrelated to any living tribe. Technically NAGPRA does
not apply.

Even so, this is a law better obeyed in the spirit than
in the letter. From the beginning Glen consulted with
Native Americans about the excavations at Windover. He
also worked with the Seminoles and Miccusukees to pass
a bill that protected grave sites years before the federal law.

Now he says simply, "Florida groups have no problem with Windover."

But that is not all he wants to say.

"With the advancing rate of technology, there are constantly good reasons to reanalyze material. What we can do now will not be as good as what we can do in five years. Or ten years. Or twenty. If we don't have the material available, then we can't do anything."

That's not quite it, either.

"I'm an osteologist, really a human biologist. There is an incredible elegance to the human skeleton. It is not a static hard compound. It can tell us things about a human's life and, in the aggregate, about a whole people's life. Outsiders don't see the emotional involvement we have with our work. These are real people. They are not statistical abstractions, not sets of interesting artifacts. They are real people."

Glen Doran could talk more about reburial. As he says, it is never far from his mind. Instead, for now, I would like to loop back to that bottle gourd, *Lagenaria siceraria,* the oldest bottle gourd in North America, dated to 5300 B.C.—the one carefully buried near the left shoulder of a thirteen-year-old girl or boy at Windover.

Useful as containers, the bottle gourd is a common early semidomesticate. Originally an Old World plant, it was probably brought to Florida by ocean currents from Africa or tropical America. I have grown bottle gourds in my own garden, as have other gardeners for thousands of years. I wonder if that's what the people at Windover were doing—growing gardens.

"These gourds don't do well without some level of human intervention," Glen says. "Left completely alone, they last about five or ten years and then disappear. Considering the complexity of people here, it's probable they were settling in. They were using looms, weaving shrouds. People don't like to move that stuff around. As they became more sedentary, it's easy for me to imagine them cultivating little plots."

Seven thousand years ago?

"Maybe," Glen says.

IN ST. LOUIS, at Washington University, Patty Jo Watson says the same thing. We are in the elegant faculty luncheon room where all the waitresses wear white aprons with black uniforms. Surreptitiously I study the kind of menu that emphasizes seasoning over substance: honey mustard with tarragon, cilantro pesto, fresh basil in cream, mango-raspberry topping. Forget the entrees. I just want the sauces.

"One thing we know," Patty Jo says, "is that agriculture begins in places like Windover where people have already been living a sedentary existence, in villages, for a long time. We used to think the opposite, that agriculture made people settle down. Now we believe they settle down first. The sedentary situation is what can set up certain social or political or environmental pressures. Maybe a population pressure. Maybe some other coercion, or combination of imperatives, that makes people want to produce more."

For a long time now, measured in a single life, Patty Jo has pursued the origins of agriculture. In 1954 she began fieldwork in Jarmo, Iraq, an early farming village. "I was raised in the Midwest," she says. "Some of my relatives are wheat and barley farmers. It made perfect sense to me to go searching for the first domesticated wheat."

The Midwest had another kind of influence. "At the same time, I grew up in a calm, benign place where there wasn't any physical challenge. No mountains, no rivers, just cornfields. Now, whatever is unknown or difficult or off the beaten track, that's what I find exciting."

In 1960 Patty Jo married "Red" Watson, a philosophy student with a degree in geology. On their honeymoon Red took Pat to a Kentucky cave he had been exploring with fellow spelunkers. When the cave was sold to the National Park Service, the spelunkers transformed themselves into a research group. In their push to legitimatize, they wanted to do archaeology. Pat Watson was their only contact.

At the time this didn't seem fortuitous. Salts Cave was littered with artifacts, but Patty Jo was preoccupied, obsessed by her work in the Near East. Still, as a nice person and a helpful wife, she asked a friend at the Illinois State Museum to come visit the cave. She recounts now what is clearly a favorite story.

"We took Joe to a place just recently discovered, called Indian Avenue. It's a longish trip, a one-quarter mile crouch, a one-quarter mile crawl, a one-half mile travel through some pretty rough passage. After that, you come out to a beautiful little place with smudges on the walls, charcoal on the floor, bits of cane, chunks of wood, a couple of paleofecal specimens. We walked this guy all the way through and back, about an eight- or ten-hour trip with packs and equipment and Coleman lanterns and so on, in the darkness, talking the whole time about research potential, this and that, having a nice conversation. When we got outside, finally, Joe turned to me and said, 'Patty, I don't *ever* want to go in there again. I'll get you money, but you have to be in charge.' Well, it turned out he had hated it!"

Patty Jo laughs. Who could hate exploring a cave? She's sixty-two years old and "When someone calls and says, let's go, I still think, Wow, yes, let's go!"

So Pat Watson became a cave archaeologist at a time when archaeologists didn't do much of that. Fortuitously now, the paleofecal specimens, dated at 500 B.C., contained the seeds of squash, gourds, sunflower, and sumpweed too big to be wild. The Indians were in the cave to mine: crystals of selenite, satin spar, gypsum for paint, mirabilite for salt. But the remains they left were like the dung of Paul Martin's Shasta ground sloths, lovely sources of dietary information. Easily then, over the coming years, Patty Jo's obsession shifted closer to home, to the origins of agriculture in eastern America.

"Everyone thought then, in 1976, that gourds and squash were introduced here from Mexico and that sunflower and sumpweed were indigenous. We wanted to know what came first. We were rooting for the latter. We wanted eastern North Americans to be cultivating their own crops early on. So we went downstream forty miles from the caves to a shell mound we knew dated to the late Archaic period. We thought we'd find some nice antecedents, some slightly smaller sunflower and sumpweed seeds. But as we floated the deposits, we didn't find any sunflower, any sumpweed, any chenopodium. Instead there were several small charred fragments of *Cucurbita pepo* gourd rind. That was a wonderful moment for me. The gourds came first! Our working hypothesis was totally, unequivocally wrong. The archaeological record had spoken. It confirmed my faith in the science of archaeology."

Later, AMS would date one of these gourds to 2500 B.C. The record had a lot more to say. Most archaeologists now think that the entire complex of eastern American crops was indigenous, including gourds and squash, excluding late arrivals like maize and beans. The news has produced little fanfare, but eastern North America is one of the world's primary food production centers, a place where people independently developed agriculture.

In a model by archaeologist Bruce Smith, the stabilization of river systems in the eastern woodlands around 5000 B.C. first allowed human settlements to increase in size and become more permanent. Wild *Cucurbita pepo* gourds, chenopod, and marsh elder began to colonize areas disturbed by human activity. Over the next few thousand years, these weedy invaders were tolerated and then encouraged. By about 2500 B.C. people were deliberately sowing beds. Competition in garden plants favors seeds that sprout and grow quickly, which in turn favors thinner seed coats and larger seeds. By 1000 B.C. crops like the sunflower were clearly the result of cultivation.

By 150 B.C. knotweed, maygrass, and little barley had been added. Maize, or corn, was also brought over from the Southwest but did not become an important crop until after A.D. 800.

In the western United States things happened differently. Around 1000 B.C. maize, squash, and beans were introduced from Mexico. Cotton and gourds followed. Even so, the hunting-and-gathering lifestyle of most people did not change much until around A.D. 200, when farmers seriously began planting crops, perhaps because of population growth or a decline in natural resources.

When the Europeans came to America in the sixteenth century, they found a land of fields and farms. Agriculture had allowed populations to further increase and provided a base for cultural complexity. Wandering through Florida in 1528 Cabeza de Vaca was reminded of Spain. "This province has many cornfields," he wrote in his journal, "and houses are scattered over the countryside as at Gelves."

Today agriculture defines our planet. It straightens our rivers, terraces our hills, and replaces our forests. By the time my lunch comes, a splendidly arrayed grilled chicken Caesar salad, I am quite aware that everything on my plate, everything on this table, everything I have ever eaten in my life is domesticated. Agriculture, simply, is who and what we are.

AGRICULTURE IS ALSO a good place to engender the past. When feminists Margaret Conkey and Joan Gero planned their 1989 conference on "Women and Production in Prehistory," they asked Patty Jo Watson to contribute a paper. Cleverly they wanted someone from the establishment, a conservative, conscientious, old-time processualist.

"Most people acknowledge that in every known society there is a sexual division of labor," Patty Jo says, "Men hunting and women gathering seems almost always to be the case. Beyond that there is tremendous variation in what kind of work a particular society assigns a particular sex. Still, the received view is that in foraging societies, men hunt animals and women gather plants."

Patty Jo is not one to casually overthrow a received view. Instead she used it as her base and "tried to do what Meg and Joan asked, to put gender into the origins of agriculture. At that point, the paper wrote itself."

With her coauthor, Mary Kennedy, she began with the work of Bruce Smith, who had emphasized a "coevolutionary approach" in which the biology of plants and people nicely intertwined. Bruce Smith believed that once humans began to sow seeds, the changes associated with domestication—larger seeds and thinner seed coats—automatically followed. In his words, this "did not require any deliberate selection efforts. All that was needed was a sustained opportunistic exploitation and minimal encouragement of what were still rather unimportant plant food sources."

Because Native American women traditionally sowed crops and collected wild plants, Pat and Mary assumed that "adult women were the chief protagonists in this horticultural drama." Their attention focused on the words "drama" and "protagonist." Bruce Smith's model was not so much wrong as dull.

"The coevolutionary formulation downplays stress, drive, intention, or innovation of any sort on the part of the people involved, in this case the women," Pat and Mary chided. "The coevolutionary approach highlights gradualness; the built-in mechanisms carry plants and people smoothly and imperceptibly from hunting-gathering-foraging to systematic harvesting to at least part-time food production with little or no effort on anyone's part. The plants virtually domesticate themselves."

If Bruce Smith ignored innovation, other archaeologists could only attribute it to men. In one theory the early cultivation of bottle gourds like those at Windover was likely done by a male shaman because "He would be the one most interested in new religious paraphernalia. He would have the greatest knowledge of plants. He would have been in communication with other shamans and probably exchanging plants and plant lore."

Patty Jo and Mary commented dryly, "We are leery of explanations that remove women from the one realm that is traditionally granted them as soon as innovation or invention enters the picture."

Innovation did not end when agriculture began. In the first millennium A.D. the farming of chenopod, knotweed, and other native plants increased in the Midwest and Midsouth, as did human population. The introduction of maize around A.D. 200 had little impact because these varieties were poorly adapted to the colder, wetter, eastern climate. Most farmers probably saw this crop as a disappointing failure. By A.D. 900, however, a hardy eight-row corn that we call Northern Flint had evolved from the original twelve-row Chaplote or Tropical Flint. Eventually the cultivation of this corn would dominate the northeastern woodlands. Archaeologists usually assume that Northern Flint was a product of climate, neglect, and plant evolution.

Patty Jo and Mary write that women in eastern America, just as likely, "actively encouraged, against environmental odds, the new starchy food source . . . it was surely the sunflower-sumpweed-chenopod gardeners in Middle and Late Woodland communities who worked, with varying success and interest, to acclimatize this imported species, by planting it deeper or shallower, earlier or later, in hills or furrows, and who crossed varieties to obtain or suppress specific traits. From about A.D. 1100 to the time of European contact, Northern Flint was the main cultivated food of the hamlets, villages, towns, and chiefdoms that arose in the Ohio River Valley and the vast region north to the Great Lakes. . . . Northern Flint, together with pumpkins, squashes, sunflowers, and a long list of other cultigens, planted, tended, harvested, and processed by women agriculturalists supported many thousands of people each year for hundreds of years. The accomplishments of these women cultivators is even more impressive when one realizes that their creation, Northern Flint, is the basis (along with Southern Dent, a maize variety that entered the southeastern United States somewhat later) for all the modern varieties of hybrid "Corn Belt Dent" grown around the world today."

Women are responsible for America's corn belt. This means something to a girl raised in the Midwest.

Like Patty Jo, like Glen Doran, it is not hard for me to imagine these female geneticists, experimenting, testing, talking to each other. The scene is as logical as it is appealing. We can send people to the moon. We can walk under water. These marvels spring from the human brain. Of course, people in the eastern woodlands were brimming with drive and innovation 3,000 years ago. Like the Paleo-Indians before them, they revved up the same human engine. For good or bad the quantum leap they made with agriculture was so high that we are still springboarding.

The authors conclude: "Based on available ethnographic evidence for the Eastern United States in particular and the sexual division of labor in general, women domesticated plants. We would like to think that they domesticated them on purpose because they were bored, or curious, or because they saw some economic advantage in it, that they acted consciously with the full powers of human intellect and that their actions were a significant contribution to culture change and to cultural elaboration. We prefer this explanation because it makes explicit a formulation that anyone who has ever studied anthropology has to some extent absorbed, i.e., that flood plants in foraging societies are women's business."

The publication of papers and the response to that is how academia works. After Patty Jo's critique appeared in the book *Engendering Archaeology,* edited by Margaret Conkey and Joan Gero, Bruce Smith replied. He agreed that his theory of plant domestication had been gender-neutral, "a previously safe and heavily populated zone of archaeological interpretation." But he cautioned against simplifying the role of gender and argued that gender-neutral approaches were not bad or biased, just "another level of analysis." He admitted that his presentation could have better acknowledged human intention. Still, he maintained that floodplain weeds like chenopod and sumpweed were preadapted to becoming garden crops; people *and* plants deserved the credit for bigger seeds and thinner seed coats.

For Bruce Smith the two viewpoints were not exclusive. Each could benefit and be modified by the other. This was the "exhilarating clash of ideas, the open and ongoing process" of "mutual criticism." Theories, after all, are supposed to shift and change.

Patty Jo believes that the feminism of *Engendering Archaeology,* now in its third printing, has already made changes. In 1985 Joan Gero pointed out that the big field grants from the National Science Foundation were going disproportionately to men. In 1991 the Society for American Archaeology formed a Committee on the Status of Women, who promptly found the usual gaps in employment, rank, and salary. Today there has been a shift in the way research questions are posed, in which questions are funded, and in which gender is funded. If this seems dated, something that should have happened earlier, it may be the fault, as Joan Gero believes, of the field's historic "cowboy" mentality. Many archaeologists, after all, liked Indiana Jones.

On her part, Patty Jo Watson never noticed any "overt sexism" in her career. Perhaps she was lucky. More likely, she was oblivious. Patty Jo's career has been a trajectory headed up and out, a plunge forward, a quick, "Yes, wow, let's go!" This is the young woman who trumpeted the call of New Archaeology in the 1960s— bold, brave days when archaeology was pure science, and science was a banner waving in the wind. When New Archaeology evolved, some stayed behind. Patty Jo went on, into caves, into feminism, into the future.

"I don't see what I'm doing now as a contradiction," she says. "It's a continuation. Lew Binford's point was that the past was accessible and the archaeological record contained what we needed to see the past. Now I'm trying to look at the record to try and see the individual. It's just another slant. When you've been working on an issue for a long time, you get bored with one approach. You want to go all around the subject. It's like a kaleidoscope. You give it another turn."

As she eats her club sandwich, Pat Watson seems kindly, down-to-earth, accessible. As one of her colleagues said, in typical archaeo-speak, she is "solidly founded in a disciplinary thought contiguous with common sense."

To return to a theme, she has her own reburial story. In 1988 geologists found the skeleton of an 8,000-year-old man in a remote Colorado cave over 10,000 feet high. The remains of the ancient cave explorer were studied for three years and then returned to a member of the Southern Ute tribe for reburial. As the lead archaeologist, Patty Jo's job was to give the bones back in an appropriate ceremony.

"I didn't have the slightest idea how to handle this," she says. "So I asked my daughter, who is a little more aware, and she said, 'A basket, Mom, put them in a basket.' So I went to Pier 1 Imports and got a really, really nice basket. Then my paleo-ethnobotanist friend suggested I wrap the bones in red cloth, which would evoke the red ocher people once used, and so I got some red silk, and that turned out to be very successful. But you know, I'm a pretty traditional archaeologist, and when I got ready to give the basket to the Southern Ute representative, he was *horrified* when he found that I had first wrapped each bone very carefully in aluminum foil. That's my schooling—conserve the data! I had to sneak quickly back into a tent and unwrap each bone, so the spirit would be released and returned to the earth, which is what he wanted.

"I learned a lot." Patty Jo says. "I believe it's important, this kind of mutual respect."

By now I am in love with this woman's life. She has a great daughter, a great husband, a great career, a great sense of humor, and a great faculty dining room. I wish I were Patty Jo Watson. These things happen so easily over lunch.

As we prepare to leave, the conclusion to our talk is a bit unsettling. "Say," Patty Jo exclaims. "Have you heard about those *Cucurbita pepo* seeds they just found at the

Page-Ladson site in Florida? They date from 10,500 B.C., and they're about ten millimeters in length. That's pretty big. The seeds from Salts Cave are only eleven or twelve millimeters long."

I try to absorb this information. "Do you mean," I ask, "that you think these Florida gourds were domesticated?"

"Well, I don't know. I'd like to think so."

Agriculture over 12,000 years ago? That changes everything. Rather it changes things a little. It screws up my chronology.

"Wait," I say, trying to catch up. "Let me get this straight."

COUNTDOWN

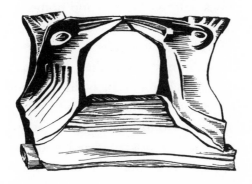

A.D.1. A PURELY ETHNOCENTRIC NUMBER. THE spotlight is on Jerusalem where we cut history in half, Before Christ and *anno Domini,* "in the year of the Lord." Archaeologists now use B.P., "Before Present," with 1950 our already dated present. But most of us, having learned the mental gymnastics of counting backwards, find it hard to think of A.D. 100 as 1850 B.P. (or of 1850 as 100 B.P.) We are pleased to have time march forward, as it seems it should, into modern life. The centuries start their countdown. It is hard to give that up, although eventually we will.

Meanwhile, in the days of Caesar, what was happening in North America? The scattered sites are few, and we can only pin labels like toy flags on a map.

In Alaska the Norton culture hunted seals, made pottery, and shaped stone into lip-plugs, lamps, and dishes. In eastern Washington the Harder phase included large pit houses, salmon fishing, and domesticated dogs. On the edge of the San Francisco Bay, Berkeley Pattern shamans were buried with kits of bone pendants and whistles. The Chumash used shell beads as a form of money. In the Great Basin nomadic hunters and gatherers had not changed much since Archaic times and would not until the European invasion. Further south, the Mogollon, Anasazi, and Hohokam were beginning to evolve. The Plains people held dramatic bison drives. A large mound-building center in the lower Mississippi Valley had peaked at 1000 B.C. and now lay in decline. Farmers in Ohio were sculpting the land with intricate, ceremonial observatories. Along the southern Atlantic Coast, pottery had been in use for 2,500 years. In northern New England it became visible just before A.D. 1.

The picture is unclear in part because it is such a big picture, filled with so many different things happening at so many different places. Timelines jump and start and from region to region seem unrelated. The patterns of ancient history swirl around geography: river and ritual, desert and detail. One thing is obvious. This country has always been multicultural.

IN THE STATE of Washington, Dale Croes offers up the Hoko River site like a gift—beloved, beribboned, sure to delight. My sister and I are traveling through the Olympic Peninsula in a nice rental car. Now we are on the dirt road that leads to Dale's cabin near Kydaka Point. He has sent me his standard two-page, single-spaced, typed guide complete with two maps. The top of the page heralds "Oh come, let us Hoko!" I read aloud the final instructions as my sister firmly handles the wheel:

> Instead of driving around the hairpin turn, continue straight ahead onto a smaller bumpier rock road and in a couple hundred feet you'll come to a locked metal gate. Obtain the combination to the lock from Dale before you leave town. Squeeze the lock to open it. Please be sure to close and lock the gate after you go through. Continuing on down the road a few hundred feet, there is another gate that is usually open. If it is closed, use the same combination on this lock and be sure to close it. The road is now narrow with high brush on each side. You are driving on top of a vacated railroad bed. You'll drive several hundred feet and come to a clearing on the right. Stay on the road and continue on down the hill. The hill at first seems very steep but really isn't bad at all. Take it slow. A three-legged deer often uses the road. Just after the steepest part, there will be a newer branch road to the right, but you will go left. Careful not to hit any rabbits . . .

Dale began excavating the Hoko River site in 1973 when he was still a graduate student. Eventually he bought a small cabin, a quarter mile away, which opens out onto a private beach of white sand, black rock, and bald eagles who come to play in the evening light glinting off the Strait of Juan de Fuca. Paradise next to a research project. Come let us Hoko.

On a wet path through the coastal woods of hemlock and spruce, we walk to the waterlogged river site one mile from the ocean. Deposits exposed on this crumbly bank include over forty layers of well-preserved vegetal mats; these contain the debris of people who came to this summer camp from 1000 B.C. to A.D. 1 to catch offshore fish and dry them for winter storage. Archaeology is often a search through garbage. Here men and women discarded thousands of pieces of broken cordage, basketry, stone, and wooden tools, as well as hundreds of bentwood and composite fishhooks, floats, and leaders.

Dale imagines a busy scene. If ten canoes with fishermen caught ten halibut a day, each weighing 15 pounds, that was 1,500 pounds of meat for the women to skin, flail, and dry. The remains of drying racks can be seen in post molds on the southern sandbar. Charcoal hearths might have kept insects away. Dale sees a scatter of shed-like structures, walled with bullrush tule mats and roofed with cedar bark. Along an upper gravel beach, a line of alder poles were staked one after another, forming runs for moving the canoes onto the bank. The air smelled of smoke, cedar, and fish. Men shouted as they brought in another load.

"The kids were by the racks, scaring away birds." Dale squints as a means of perfecting his vision. "Everyone was busy in camp, splitting firewood, splitting planks, adzing canoes, weaving pack baskets. The women were making clothes, making tule mats, making bark bags, preparing food, nursing babies, smoking halibut. They wore cedar-bark skirts and capes. Some people had on hats."

Thousands of years later these hats are still important. They came in two styles, knobtop and flattop. In precontact and early historic time, knobtop hats belonged to the noble class. Commoners wore flattops. Up and down the Northwest Coast, social ranking was clearly part of life by A.D. 1000. Commoners were associated with noble families who owned hunting and fishing rights to every stream and meadow. Slaves were another form of property that could be bought, sold, destroyed, or damaged; they probably made up 10 to 25 percent of the population. The rules varied from tribe to tribe, and warfare between groups could be fierce. Ceremonies like the potlatch, in which headmen or Big Men gave away piles of goods, served to validate the social order. A potlatch might establish the succession of a new chief, announce a marriage alliance, or redistribute food. At Hoko River the presence of knobtops and flattops means that social stratification may have begun here as early as 1000 B.C.

The Northwest Coast is famous for abundance: candlefish so rich in oil they can be dried and lit for evening light, salmon packed into silver roads of flesh. Given such bounty, why did these hunters and gatherers evolve into hierarchies of knobtops, flattops, and slaves? As one archaeologist put in, were coastal Big Men "functional or fungal?"

Dale Croes likes computers. In one cultural model—having plugged in the environmental and archaeological data, factoring in social goals that range from getting enough food to maintaining a sexual division of labor—he has computed a pattern. He sees the development of the Northwest Coast as a series of economic strategies designed to deal with population growth.

For example, fifty men and women on the Olympic Peninsula in 7000 B.C., multiplying at a low .1 percent annually, produce a population of 7,500 by 2000 B.C. and 24,000 by 1000 B.C. Despite the area's wealth, people had to deal with occasional scarcity—a bad fishing season, a poor berry crop. These fluctuations combined with an over-use of natural resources to inspire the more efficient use of resources and a better storage system. People learned to make smokehouses, drying racks, baskets, and watertight boxes. This storage economy allowed for further population growth, with social groups becoming more sedentary and territorial. The ownership of territories encouraged personal status. The competition for territories encouraged the leadership required for war and trade. Most importantly these leaders helped manage an increasingly intensive, sustainable system of harvesting and preserving food.

In the end the Northwest Coast had the most complex societies of any hunters and gatherers we know and a very high population density. In a positive feedback loop, each technical or social adaptation to resource stress increased the area's human-carrying capacity, which resulted in more people, which required a further technical or social response. Human psychology—ambition and greed—probably influenced the form of adaptation. Headmen were both necessary and opportunistic.

This may be the way of things. In *The Evolution of Human Societies,* Allen Johnson and Timothy Earle write, "The primary motor for cultural evolution is population growth." The small independent family camp of ten to thirty members is where we are "biologically most comfortable" and "best equipped." Families struggle to maintain their autonomy. They form larger groups only when increasing population leads to resource depletion and warfare. As that stress increases, these local groups make alliances managed by Big Men. Organized technology, such as irrigation or storage, allows for an even larger population. A step up from Big Men is the chiefdom. Invested with special powers, descended from gods, chiefs develop a cadre of elites who control outlying resources that bring in even more income. Public ceremonies legitimize inequity and "provide a kind of social glue."

The state follows. "Integration at this level is beyond the informal control of a hereditary elite. It requires a state bureaucracy, a state religion, a judiciary, and a police force." Further stratification is inevitable. Our own "socialistic and democratic alternatives only decorate a fundamental stratification with an ideology of egalitarianism."

Timothy Earle sees this as a cultural spiral. With each turn the family unit rebels. We yearn for our original freedom when the land was young and we traveled across the plains bound to each other by trust and blood. For these authors, however, "The steady increase in population density that underlies cultural evolution creates problems that only the group can solve or, at least, that the group can solve most efficiently." The family's survival becomes less and less possible outside this group. We come together as a society not because we want to but because we must.

Typically archaeology raises more questions than it answers. By A.D. 2020 world population could reach 8 billion. Can the group solve this problem efficiently or at all? Furthermore, in a nation-state decorated with the ideology of democracy, we still wonder: functional or fungal? Is social ranking always necessary? Are there new ideas ahead—or behind us?

For clearly the spiral is too simple a shape. Cultures and evolution can go in any direction—backwards, forwards, sideways. With hindsight a better analogy may emerge, in another 10,000 years.

Hoko River was a place of both natural and created beauty. From this site comes North America's oldest wooden artwork, a red-cedar mat creaser used to crush tule stems. The creaser's handle has been carved into the image of two kingfishers, their beaks delicately touching in the middle. It can stand for the glory of art that dominates the Northwest cultures: beautifully decorated canoes and paddles, painted cedar boxes, gorgeous masks, monumental totem poles, intricately carved spoons, rattles, clubs, and pipes. The world is transformed. Bowls are bears. Helmets are ravens. Religious theater was also well developed. In the early eighteenth century mythical dreams were still performed by secret societies. Trapdoors and hidden passages allowed actors to appear and disappear. Hollow kelp stems served as microphones.

At times the images of the Northwest can seem unremittingly fierce. Animals grin happily with full sets of large white teeth. Danger and death. Watch out! This is the art of hunters and gatherers.

It is also the art of social complexity. Chiefs sought out commoners who were good at making baskets or painting boxes. People could specialize. Ceremonial art was valued; public art was subsidized. We can trace a line from population growth to opera. The greater our number, the greater our creativity (if we are allowed to create, if we are all fed).

Dale Croes offers Hoko River like a gift. Along the wet crumbly bank, he shows us the colors of vegetal mats. In one lower layer a piece of cordage is embedded in dark-brown mud. This was made by human beings 3,000 years ago. I touch it lightly. I am thrilled.

Up the bank into the dripping forest, Dale rips a root from the bottom of a spruce tree. He peels and twists it into string which he ties as a bracelet around my sister's wrist. "Cordage," Dale says prosaically. "It's incredibly strong. They used it to sew tule mats, and they needed hundreds of feet to make one tule mat shelter. This would be another good job for the kids, sitting around, peeling, twisting spruce roots."

Later that evening Dale makes us fish-head stew. He is mildly disappointed there aren't more fishheads with their cold dead eyes staring up from the potatoes and corn. Dale has a mischievous nature. He likes to watch people eat slimy food from the sea. At sunset the eagles discuss territory on the beach. My sister and I gather quartz, which Dale chips into small, sharp flakes.

"These would be inset into hafts of split-cedar wood handles," he explains. "Like handy X-acto knives, perfect for flaying halibut. The descendants of these people, the Makah women today, are very possessive about their fish knives. I'm pretty sure the women at Hoko did their own flint knapping."

In the darkness the sky becomes the ocean. A bar of white glows, crashes, disappears, reappears. Dale has sat here many times with his students from the university and with high school groups. He tells funny stories about working with the Makahs, trying to duplicate ancient fishing techniques.

At the Seattle Aquarium they made composite hooks and dangled them into the water. "The Pacific cod would strike hard, breaking the hooks exactly as we find them in the Hoko site. So we realized that these hooks were probably designed for flatfish instead. The bent-wood hooks are for the more aggressive cod. None of this hurt the fish at the aquarium. They just spit the hooks out. But there was a boy watching us and he kept tugging at his mother, who wasn't paying any attention. 'Mom, they're fishing in there. Mom, they're *fishing* in there!' Naah, she would shrug. Naaaah."

The next morning, at low tide, the three of us meet again to gather chitons, sea urchins, and acorn barnacles.

Dale wants to take these to his friend Isabell Ides, a ninety-five-year-old Makah at Neah Bay. Working in a light rain on Kydaka Point, Dale builds a small fire over a patch of barnacles. The heat kills them, and they loosen their grip. "We would never know how to do this," he says, giving us some of the nutty-tasting meat, "if we hadn't started talking to the Makah elders. They're invaluable."

Catching chitons is tricky. These primitive oval-shaped mollusks, about two inches long, creep lugubriously over the wet rocks. Using a sharpened stick, I must dislodge them on the first try before they dig in with the full force of their powerful bottom foot. Dale claims that his Makah friends eat chiton feet as a kind of chewing gum. He pops one in his mouth.

"Try it," he urges.

"It's alive," I object.

"No, not any longer," he says. "At least, I don't think so." I try to chew the creature in such a way that no part of my mouth actually touches it. Later my sister confesses that she put her chiton back in the water. When Dale isn't looking I hide mine in my pocket.

At Dale's cabin we eat a huge pancake breakfast before going off to gather Sitka sedge. These long flexible leaves, with a ridge down the middle, will be split in half, dried, bleached in the sun, dyed, and woven into baskets. It is still raining, drizzling, dreaming in the forest. Shades of green shimmer and hum: ferns, salal, devil's claw, spruce, and hemlock. Elsewhere on the Olympic Peninsula giant red cedars rise up above this dense undergrowth, their thick straight trunks seeking the light.

These woods do not mimic cathedrals; cathedrals are built to mimic them. Like most Native Americans, tribal groups in the Northwest believed that the natural world was sacred. Of course they did. Only a fool would stand in the middle of this beauty and think otherwise. I am convinced of few things, and that list grows shorter as I grow older. Still, I am convinced that people who do not admit the sacred power of the natural world are behaving foolishly.

With our pails of leaves and shellfish, Dale Croes takes my sister and me to Isabell's house on the Makah Reservation. First we visit some of his friends at Neah Bay, most of whom are related to Isabell. One man is carving a totem pole commissioned by David Melznick, the Hollywood producer. Inside a trailer his wife shows us a half-finished basket. Dale says he is taking Isabell some Sitka sedge. The woman nods. She also takes things to Isabell. As Dale jokes and greets the children who come into the trailer asking for cereal, he is giving us the web of this community, his greatest discovery.

Twenty-three years ago Dale took a class from Isabell and learned enough to make a few baskets for his mother and grandmother. He also began a relationship nurtured for personal as well as professional reasons. We claim community whenever we can. As an archaeologist, Dale strongly supports the rights of Native Americans to control and monitor archaeological research. "It's more than working closely together," he corrects me at one point. "This is a *joint* project." For Dale Croes the Makahs are not only partners; they are senior partners.

In the Northwest social complexity has helped keep tradition alive, embedded in art. The forest is still sacred. Lineage is still remembered. Local author Ruth Kirk writes, "Even today, people are aware of family members lost to slavery generations ago. . . . A young Makah woman remarked, 'I know who the slave families are and someday my baby daughter will know too.' Another commented, 'I'm tired of all this about who is slave and who is chief. That kind of talk divides us, and we need to pull together. We have bigger problems.' "

When Dale goes to potlatches he watches his friends behave in ways that connect them directly to their ancestors. He likes to bring his own son. He enjoys the Makahs' sense of humor.

"Years ago," he tells my sister, "a friend of mine was taking some Makah elders home from the World's Fair in Spokane. They were in the back of the van, but my friend wanted to check on the suitcases. 'Wait,' he said. 'Are all the bags in the back?' The women began laughing. 'Yes, all us old bags are back here!' They never let him forget that. At every potlatch since, this guy hands out plastic bags with presents, sometimes hundreds of pounds of fish for them, as a kind of payment."

That afternoon, at last, we arrive at Isabell's house, a center place, small, modest, surrounded by ocean and forest. Here the gifts flow in and out. Earlier we had stopped at a grocery store, where Dale suggested we buy Isabell onions and a carton of ice-cream. Now he gives her the pail of chitons, sea urchins, and mussels. Isabell looks exactly as you imagine her to look. She receives her presents graciously, exclaiming over the ice cream, grinning at the sea urchins. She shows us the salmon in her smokehouse, and we eat some of the crunchy, salty meat. She shows us her baskets, lined on a shelf, ready for sale to tourists and art collectors. Outside on the ground, we sit and split in half the leaves of Sitka sedge. Dale asks Isabell to tell a story. This is her gift to us.

"Bear," she begins with ease and enjoyment, "invited Raven to eat salmon at his house."

IN PHOENIX, ARIZONA, the Pueblo Grande Museum and Cultural Park is on 44th and Washington Street, near the Hohokam Freeway, the immense Sky Harbor Airport, a railroad track, and a bar that advertises topless waitresses. The 100-acre site includes the remains of Pueblo Grande, with its ancient platform mound, ball court, and canal system. Visitors here feel a strange dissonance as jets roar through the sky and trains shake the ground. The adobe ruins stand mutely. It is tacky to anthropomorphize, but they seem confused.

By A.D. 1 Hohokam people in the Sonoran Desert were irrigating crops, making pottery, and living in villages. Most archaeologists believe the Hohokam evolved from the Southwestern Archaic culture; a few scholars see them as migrants from Mexico. Eventually these men and women built large pit houses that encircled central plazas. They made a red-on-buff pottery and fashioned small clay figurines decorated with earrings, cheek plugs, tattoos, and turbans. They grew cotton, squash, beans, and corn. They carved and etched shells into unique ornaments, which they traded widely. Certainly they were exposed to Mesoamerican ideas. Stone palettes and censers imply an elaborate death ritual. By A.D. 1000 they also had a network of ball courts that extended more than 150 miles north and south. Their irrigation systems were the most complex in North America with canals up to ninety feet wide diverting water as much as seventeen miles from the Salt River.

Around A.D. 1100 certain Hohokam towns were abandoned while others prospered. The cremation of the dead and the practice of some crafts declined. As fewer ball courts were built, large platform mounds took their place. Here, on top, a few people put their homes and surrounded them with private compound walls. At Pueblo Grande a mound as large as a football field and twenty-five feet high may have been built in phases with generations of help. During the Classic Period, after A.D. 1100, 1,000 people could have lived in this village to help manage ten working canals, which irrigated some 20,000 acres. Even so, the population appeared to suffer from malnutrition.

In 1358 and 1380–82 large floods on the Salt River probably destroyed much of this irrigation system. In one Pima legend Elder Brother leads a revolt against "the evil chiefs who rule ontop the platform mounds." This also suggests increased warfare or a dissatisfaction with the religious leadership. For whatever reasons, by 1500 the

Hohokam had deserted Pueblo Grande and other villages in the Phoenix and Tucson area. Their canals silted in. Their houses collapsed. Their mounds eroded.

Todd Bostwick, archaeologist for the city of Phoenix, has his office in the back of the Pueblo Grande Museum, with a window overlooking the parking lot and a few spires of saguaro. I grew up in this town. While the forests of the Olympic Peninsula are exotic to me, prickly pear and saguaro cactus are not. My definition of beauty still revolves around the arboreal desert. At the same time, I have always disliked the cancerous sprawl of central Arizona. When Todd tells me that Phoenix recently won an international award for "The Best Managed City in the World," I am amazed. In part, the jurors were impressed by the Pueblo Grande Museum and the attention paid here to archaeology. This is Todd's job, paying attention to archaeology in a city entranced with perpetual development, a city built directly on the villages, canals, homes, mounds, and ball courts of the Hohokam.

"Sites are everywhere," Todd says. "Phoenix doesn't have an ordinance that deals directly with archaeology, but we have a stringent state law that mimics and supports federal law. I depend on that."

Under the National Historic Preservation Act of 1966, projects on federal land or that require a federal permit must first survey for archaeological sites before the area is disturbed. Sites that are found and deemed significant are then avoided or excavated under the guidance of NAGPRA and other laws. Typical projects range from highways to stock tanks in the national forest. Under state laws in Arizona, any private landowner or agency who uncovers human remains or burial artifacts must leave them undisturbed and notify the Arizona State Museum. Officials quickly consult with local tribes. Usually construction can continue around the material. Otherwise it must be excavated and returned to those tribes who claim a cultural affiliation. It is a crime to sell human remains or any items buried with them.

A Phoenix developer or contractor who finds himself digging up a grave first calls Todd Bostwick. Todd has two working days to contact Lynn Teague at the Arizona State Museum. "But I call her within minutes," Todd says. "We try to work with business people, to be flexible. Their concern is how this is going to impact their schedule. I have project managers quoting me numbers all the time about what a one-day delay is going to cost, and it's mind-boggling. At first, I didn't believe them. Pretty soon I realized they were only slightly exaggerating. These are figures of $50,000–$200,000 daily.

"The builder often wants to do as little archaeology as possible, and I want to do as much as possible, and we find the balance," Todd says. "Fortunately, most schedule changes can be avoided, especially when archaeology is considered from the very beginning. In planning a project, archaeology should be just another check-off on the list. These are the rules now. This is the law. I serve mainly as a consultant. I help hire other archaeologists who will do the work. In recent years, I've seen developers become more resigned—and more interested. A lot of people in Arizona consider this heritage to be very important. A lot of tourists do too. I can appeal to other agency managers and to some private landowners on a personal level. I try to make them feel good about what they're doing."

Todd wears many hats and changes them rapidly as he answers the phone. He talks to artists, journalists, city officials, developers, construction workers, and CEOs. He is in charge of preserving the Pueblo Grande ruins and expanding the museum. He deals directly with the five tribes who claim affinity to the Hohokam.

"I'm a clearing house. Yesterday I got a call to go to the airport because they found some bones while doing construction. The detectives wanted to know if this was an old body or a new body. In the end, I could tell them it was a pig or a dog, possibly a Hohokam dog, but not a human being.

"I have to respond and react to so many levels of individuals and agencies. I have to be a politician, careful of what I say and how I say it. I have to monitor myself. It's good to be conscious and to construct my statements in a clear and thoughtful way," Todd says, carefully.

In odd moments he does archaeology. His research compares the Hohokam platform mounds with southeastern mounds from the same time period. The latter were "objects of sacred display, periodically rebuilt and remodeled as a community death and rebirth ritual." Todd wonders if ball courts and platform mounds were not competing ceremonial systems. He looks south to the Aztecs whose pyramids symbolized sacred mountains, the source of water. Hohokam mounds correlate with the distribution of saguaro cactus, and Southwestern Indians still associate rain with the fermentation of saguaro wine. Todd thinks that Hohokam mound ceremonies were also related to rain, as well as flood control. That might explain the area's abandonment after the floods of the fourteenth century. It wasn't just the canal system that failed.

Todd sees a parallel with Mesoamerican religion, which has been described as world making, the creation of myths that describe the origin of the universe; world centering, the relationship of those myths to the human body; and world renewing, the ceremonial rejuvenation of this cosmic order. Aztec cities were modeled after a vision of the universe. The Aztecs centered their world by linking human sacrifice with the movement of the sun. They renewed the world through constant public ritual and performance.

In Phoenix, at Pueblo Grande, astronomical observation and cycles of time also were important enough to be built into the architecture. Platform mounds had a formal relationship within villages and among villages. Many artifacts involved ritual, including possible bloodletting and the use of scarification tools.

"I think archaeology should pay more attention to religion," Todd says. "We see the world as inanimate. They saw it as animate. There is an enormous gap between the secular and the sacred, between the way they knew their place in the universe and the way we don't. A 'closeness to nature' doesn't begin to explain the difference.

"Can we bridge that? In part, I think so. I read a lot of ethnography and religious studies, and I go out in the desert, and I have an insight, and I see things differently."

Todd is putting on a new hat, one I haven't seen before. I wonder what insights he has in the desert. I wonder what can bridge the Hohokam and the Hohokam Freeway, beyond the fact that both represent technical achievement, the management of too many people in the desert. When I ask Todd more about his "religious studies," I naturally feel a little shy, like most Americans, like most archaeologists. There is an enormous gap between the secular and the sacred.

Unfortunately it is not a gap that Todd and I will cross today. The phone rings. Someone has a problem.

We, too, keep a close watch on cycles of time, which are measured quite strictly in today's working world. Todd picks up the receiver. My time is up.

OHIO IS A GREEN BOX. Obviously this isn't true. The sky has no hinge, and the sky is blue, not green. Even so, in this bountiful May, surrounded by lush fields, rolling hills, and screens of hardwood forests, I feel as though I have been transported from a dry land and released to live here, forever, in a green box.

Nearly 200 years ago visitors to the Midwest saw similar green fields, hills, and forests. They also saw mounds, as many as 10,000 near the Ohio River and its tributaries. They walked beside massive geometric earthworks: octagons, hexagons, circles, rectangles. They discovered huge animals rising up from the ground: snakes, birds, turtles. They saw a landscape sculpted, molded like clay by human hands to fit some vision of the human mind.

In 1820 Caleb Atwater published his map of the Newark Earthworks in Newark, Ohio. They included a circle whose four-foot-high walls enclosed twenty acres and joined an octagon that surrounded fifty acres, which were connected by a mile-long corridor to a square that opened south to another circle, via a broad passageway, and north to an oval through disjointed corridors. Atwater believed this singular design, covering four square miles, was an ancient fort. His map highlighted certain "military" features and omitted others that did not fit his interpretation. In 1848 Ephraim G. Squier and Edwin H. Davis resurveyed the site. Their map had many new corridors, walls, and enclosures. They found the "earthworks so complicated that it is impossible to give anything like a comprehensible description of them." They also mourned the rapid destruction of the area from plowing and development.

In his history of archaeology Bruce Trigger writes, "These earthworks, which often contained elaborate artifacts made of pottery, shell, mica, and native copper, challenged the belief that native American cultures were invariably primitive." Although some nineteenth-century scientists believed that Native Americans built the earthworks, many others attributed them to the Danes, Vikings, Toltecs, or Welsh, "a race of Moundbuilders who were imagined to have been destroyed or driven out of

North America by savage hordes. . . . The archaeological record was interpreted as further evidence of the menace posed by the Indians, who were revealed to be destroyers of civilization when given the opportunity."

The mounds of Ohio were mysterious in part because men like Caleb Atwater saw a real discrepancy between the historic numbers of American Indians and their "cultural level" and the abundance and sophistication of the Moundbuilder remains. At that time European-Americans could hardly imagine the horror of the sixteenth and early seventeenth century, when whole tribes were wiped out by diseases brought with early Spanish explorers. With that in mind one archaeologist has described Bruce Trigger's story of eighteenth- and nineteenth-century scholars as a "twentieth-century story about eighteenth- and nineteenth-century scholars."

In any case we now know that the Newark Earthworks were built during the second of three major moundbuilding phases in ancient America. The first had been in the lower Mississippi Valley from 1500 to 700 B.C., where six-foot-high concentric semi-circles face a central plaza at Poverty Point. As many as 5,000 people lived in this village. Later, from 500 B.C. to A.D. 400, what we call the Adena-Hopewell flourished in central and southern Ohio. Later still, the Mississippian culture built mounds throughout the Southeast from A.D. 900 to 1500.

Around A.D. 1, the Ohio Hopewell had a vast trade network: hammered copper from the Great Lakes; chert, ceramic figures, soapstone pipes, and flint from the Midwest; mica from Appalachia; obsidian and bear teeth from the Rocky Mountains; shark teeth, alligator teeth, barracuda jaws, and turtle shells from the Gulf of Mexico. These tall vigorous people probably lived in scattered hamlets and practiced extensive horticulture with little or no corn. Their elaborate earthworks and style of mound-building, their mortuary customs, their artwork and religious beliefs spread up to the Great Lakes and down to Florida, creating a Hopewellian "sphere of influence" that lasted for centuries.

Even so, Hopewell archaeology has been relatively unsung, underfunded, and underresearched.

In *Native Americans Before 1492: The Moundbuilding Centers of the Eastern Woodlands,* Lynda Norene Shaffer comments, "The people of Eastern North America were and are located upon the stage where the early history of this nation was enacted, and they, too, had a part in the drama. Thus to know their history, before and after 1492, and to consider it to be a part of our own would require a complete reconstruction of our understanding of the very foundations of our nation. No doubt, it is for this reason that it has always been easier to forget those who lived in the Eastern Woodlands and to romanticize those who lived in the West."

Still, "To know truly who we are and to be at peace with this knowledge, we must be willing to claim all of our national ancestors, winners of the day and losers too, and we must claim all of our siblings and cousins. We must know their names and their relationships to us. Then we can celebrate the existence of all of us now within the bounds of the United States, and especially the survival of those nations who were here when Columbus sailed."

At the Moundbuilders State Memorial Museum, in the middle of Newark, in the center of one of its two circles, Brad Lepper explains further why Hopewell archaeology has been neglected. "It's just harder to do archaeology in the East. It's wet and green and everything gets covered up. Also, in the West there is a lot of public land. Here you almost always have to deal with private landowners. These owners have been plowing their land for centuries. There is the misperception that all the sites are gone."

Like Todd, Brad's job as curator of the Newark Earthworks gives him little time to do research. But he has used his little time well—to find the earliest known road in North America.

"It began when I was looking at those old maps and records. Caleb Atwater wrote that parallel walls leave the octagon and might go as much as thirty miles south. Squier and Davis said these walls only went two and one-half miles south. But in 1861 James Salisbury and his brother actually traced these walls, crossed a creek, and followed them for another six miles. Then they turned back, not because they found the end of the walls but because they were tired or bored or who knows what." Brad pauses. "Sometimes I wish I could go back in a time travel machine and yell at them. 'Keep going! Keep going!' "

"Instead I took a protractor and a dozen or so quadrangle maps and extended the line from Newark. It pointed to the heart of Chilicothe, sixty miles to the south. As an undergraduate student I had seen the roads at Chaco Canyon in New Mexico, straight roads too, sometimes with masonry walls defining them. And I wondered if we didn't have the same kind of road here. Then I found several aerial photographs that showed two lines cutting the farmland here and there between Newark and Chilicothe, where the Hopewell built the only other circle and octagon we know of. The circle in Chilicothe is exactly the same size as the one here. Also, Newark's circle and octagon are lined up to the northern-most rise of the moon, and the Chilicothe circle and octagon is lined up to the southern-most rise of the moon. These two sites are connected by geometry, astronomy, and, maybe, a physical roadway!"

Brad envisions a set of parallel walls about 200 feet apart. At Newark the walls started off grandly, three feet high. Elsewhere they may have been lower. In 1992 the Ohio Department of Transportation lent Brad a helicopter. From the sky he could see more signs of his road in just the right places. At the outskirts of Chilicothe, he spotted telltale soil stains. Engineered and built at the time of the Romans, the Great Hopewell Road had been found.

In Brad Lepper's tiny office, maps of the Newark earthworks cover the wall above his desk. The intricate design is mesmerizing, possibly addictive.

"It's like looking at a hieroglyph," Brad says, "a symbol I know is pregnant with a meaning I'll never completely grasp. If we had any literature for this, I'm sure it would be as complex as the Egyptian Book of the Dead." He points to one of the circles. "There are only three ways in and out of this area: here, here, and here. Movement was channeled in very specific ways. The circles are cul-de-sacs, while the octagons have multiple exits."

Brad studies the map afresh, as though he has not studied it until the lines are permanently etched onto his retina. He can see this hieroglyph in the dark. He describes a ceremony that begins, perhaps, in Chilicothe, sixty miles south of Newark. There, accompanied by a huge crowd, priests stand at one end of the circle and octagon and sight through parallel walls to see the moon rise at its southern-most point. That lunar standstill (when the moon stays at this point a few days) will not happen for another 18.6 years. In 9.3 years, the priests will wait at one end of the circle and octagon in Newark, sight through the parallel walls, and see the moon rise at its northern-most point.

"Issac Newton said that the cycles of the moon are the only math problem that gave him a headache," Brad says. "I have problems with that math too. But the Hopewell didn't have a problem. They had people as smart as Issac Newton. I don't think they were coldly making astronomical observations and calculations. But the cycles of the heavens were very important to them, and they were bringing those cycles down to the earth and incorporating them in their architecture. . . . For us, you know, as soon as we are old enough to wonder about the moon, we are told that it's a big rock orbiting our planet. We are robbed of some mystery at a very early age. What should be this glorious, awesome spectacle is, well, less glorious. But for the Hopewell, this was the nightly show and entertainment.

"These earthworks were probably many things, a kind of cathedral or Vatican, an astronomical observatory, a trading center or shopping mall, an important burial place, a place of social gathering. Every nine years is a good time to get together as a big group to see who has reached marriageable age or to visit relatives who have moved away. The road was part of this interaction and ceremony."

Besides geometric earthworks, the Hopewell also built hilltop enclosures. "Instead of finding a flat plain and imposing on it some complex geometry," Brad says, "they went to a high inaccessible hill and built walls that conformed to the contours of the hilltop. It took an incredible amount of labor. Maybe the people who did this were a different religious sect. Maybe they went to these enclosures at different times of the year, to get closer to the sky. I don't have a good answer. It's all mysterious.

"Whenever we find this kind of monumental architecture, we also find a state-level society, a hierarchy. But I don't see that here. We do see the burials of important leaders. But we don't see inherited status, with power passed down to children. I think the Hopewell were relatively egalitarian. Given that, how do you sustain this kind of labor, this vision, across generations without any kind of written language or centralized authority?"

By A.D. 500 the Hopewellian phenomenon was gone. No human vision is sustained indefinitely. Brad

wonders if outsiders came and outcompeted the Hopewell, or if the population grew to the point where the
villages were competing with each other. Some archaeologists believe that the trade network fell apart when
southerners, who had exchanged coastal shells for northern copper, discovered their own copper. Then again,
that may have been a result, not a cause, of the decline in
moundbuilding. Possibly the bow and arrow, introduced
around A.D. 300, altered the balance of power. Certainly
warfare became more common at this time, and the next
phase of moundbuilding would be less gentle.

Leaving Brad's office, I take a walk on top of the
embankment of the Great Circle. Trees close over my
head, and birds move secretly in the brush. I feel excited—jazzed. When I walk through a forest, I want to be
what I am not, to merge with what is instinctive and wild.
But I fancy that the Hopewell were profoundly different.
They walked through a forest and dreamed of separation.
They wanted to assert their humanity, and they succeeded
in a way that is deeply, aesthetically satisfying.

To get to the octagon and second circle, I must enter
the fray of Newark traffic. Brad draws me a map which
becomes my own hieroglyph. Finally I park near a homey
but expensive-looking building called The Moundbuilders Country Club. Brad has warned me about this.
The Ohio Historical Society leases this second archaeological site to a privately owned golf course. "It's a unique
way of preserving the earthworks," Brad said, looking
shifty. "Right," I agreed without thinking. Now I am
confused. Near the parking lot I climb a wooden tower,

which gives me an overview of the circle and octagon. Two grassy parallel embankments rise in front of me, and I can see other high walls quite a distance away. But mostly I see people playing golf. Tiny golf carts veer along tiny golf cart paths. Putting circles stand out brown against the green. Flags wave in the spring breeze.

Suddenly the shapes make sense. The two parallel walls are the corridor that connects the octagon to the circle. Far to the left is where the circle begins and the priests once stood to calculate the northern-most rise of the moon. Right now a tiny figure is teeing off. The walls of the octagon and circle actually define the borders of this golf course. The entire site has become a golf course.

I am stunned. I wait for a wave of indignation. It rises, falters, falls back. My powers of indignation are stunned. Perhaps it is the dead-seriousness with which people play golf. This business of getting a small white ball into a small dark hole seems to warrant a concentration that outweighs the silliness of the game. The men and women of Ohio stride purposefully across the manicured green. I watch amazed while Americans putt in the sacred circle.

The feeling of being an anthropologist in my own culture is not unfamiliar. What *are* these people thinking? For a moment I can almost understand the Hopewell better.

BRIGHT LIGHTS, BIG CITY

MONKS MOUND AT CAHOKIA MOUNDS STATE
Park in Illinois is the largest earthwork in the Western
Hemisphere: 100 feet tall, 700 feet wide, 1,000 feet long.
Squat, immobile, like some giant brooding toad, the flat-
topped pyramid covers over fourteen acres. If I had stood
here on top in A.D. 1150, I would have seen one of the
great urban centers of my time. The downtown area includes this mound, a large plaza with a playing field, some
sixteen other mounds, and a busy marketplace, all enclosed by a two-mile-long palisade with watch towers every seventy feet. Outside the wall are 100 more mounds,

charnel houses, sweat lodges, granaries, menstrual huts, alleys, neighborhoods, and an impressive circle of wooden posts which serve me as a solar calendar. Perhaps 20,000 people live in my diamond-shaped city. No one, however, lives in a grander house than mine, the central eye of the diamond, set like a jewel in the toad's forehead. From this point I can turn in a circle and see nothing that is higher or better.

On Monks Mound boasting comes naturally. A Sun King would have felt like a Sun King here, close to the sky, above everyone else. That was probably the point.

Today the view is serenely rural. The grandeur of Cahokia has been replaced by the grassy fields of this state park with its remaining mounds bordered by trailers and suburban debris. To the west, the Great Arch of St. Louis rises amid a retinue of skyscrapers. Nothing, they seem to boast, is higher or better.

In their third mound building phase, A.D. 900 to 1500, the people we call Mississippians built many kinds of earthworks. The home of the current ruler often stood on top of a platform mound that faced a central plaza. When this chief died, the palace was destroyed before a new layer of earth and a new palace were added. Conical and ridge-topped mounds more often contained the burials of the elite. The height of a palace mound may have been a measure of the length of a chief's lineage, with the number of conical and ridge-topped mounds indicating families who had allied themselves with the chief. If so, anyone approaching such a center could easily judge the strength of its ruling lineage.

The politics of lineage began with the fertility of corn. For the Hopewell, tropical flint corn had been a poor crop, used mainly in ceremony. But with the development of new varieties, the rich soil of the Midwest supported a rapid increase in population. By A.D. 1000 Mississippians were dependent on the agriculture of maize and beans. By A.D. 1150—roughly the time of the Crusades in Europe and the Toltec empire in Mexico— Cahokia was at its peak, thriving, populous, byzantine. Some archaeologists balk at the descriptive term "city," yet Cahokia fits every definition of urban life, except for its lack of a written language.

One of many towns along the Mississippi River, Cahokia was the largest, with its own suburbs, outlying villages, and farms. The bow and arrow remained as important as the hoe. People still hunted, fished, gathered wild plants, and dug for roots. In their leisure they gambled with dice and were obsessed with a game called chunkey in which two players threw javelins at a rolling stone. Trade was extensive. Artwork was distinct. In etched shell and hammered copper, Cahokian dancers are dressed in elaborate bird costumes, men and women kneel reverently, and warriors stare with hawklike eyes. Circles with crosses, the sun, and the human eyeball are common symbols.

Around A.D. 1200 Cahokia began to decline. As the surrounding fields and woods became depleted, the city may have been forced into a dependence on other regions. A colder climate probably affected agriculture. For a long time, too, the population had suffered from a diet too high in carbohydrates and too low in protein. Small stones in the cornmeal damaged teeth, infants died frequently, and malnutrition was common. Woodsmoke and human waste polluted the inner neighborhoods. Disease flourished in these crowded conditions; tuberculosis, in particular, may have become a plague. Urban stress was the latest invention, and by A.D. 1400 Cahokia had been abandoned.

Elsewhere other centers rose to prominence, although none would ever be as large or as magnificent. Native Americans in the Southeast continued to build mounds and palisaded towns—and to depend on corn. Modern descendants of the Mississippian tradition include the Choctaw, Cherokee, Chickasaw, Creek, Shawnee, Seminole, and Muscasokee. When Spanish explorers came in the sixteenth century, they met people whose customs probably echoed those of the Cahokians. Journals written between 1539 and 1543 on the Hernando de Soto expedition describe a countryside of fields and villages surrounded by stockades. Below the powerful chiefs known as Great Suns were various classes of "notables," "principal men," and "commoners." In most cases status came through the mother. Hernando de Soto even had the privilege of meeting a "woman chief, lady of that land whom Indians of rank bore on their shoulders with much respect, in a litter covered with delicate white linen."

In the eighteenth century, on the banks of the Mississippi, the French met and warred with the Natchez, who were still ruled by a royal lineage that claimed descent from the sun. Natchez commoners never turned their backs on *le Roi Soleil,* who was treated with extreme deference. In 1731 after the Natchez attacked a trading post, they were crushed by an alliance of the French and Choctaw. Four hundred survivors, including the Great Sun, were sold into slavery in the West Indies. That is a story the imagination continues, the fall of a deity, a cosmos overturned.

At Cahokia the ruins were named for the Cahokia Indians living in the area. In the early 1800s French Trappist Monks settled here and planted gardens on what would be called Monks Mound. In 1925 the state of Illinois created Cahokia Mounds State Park. Sixty-four years later, the park was declared a UNESCO World Heritage Site, one of three archaeological sites in the United States. (The other two are Chaco Canyon and Mesa Verde.) An interpretive center, built for over 8 million dollars, highlights a prize-winning multimedia show, a recreated village with life-sized models, a series of spectacular murals and views, state-of-the-art exhibits, and an enormous front door with bronze panels and bas-relief designs. Taped music and conversation plays softly in the background. A flute trills. Women talk as they grind corn. This is, perhaps, a perfect museum.

On top of Monks Mound a thousand years ago, I would have seen in one glance hundreds of people: merchants, artisans, priests, chunkey players, soldiers, commoners, bakermen, thieves. This afternoon I see hundreds of school children, for it is Kids Day at Cahokia Mounds State Park, and the children are everywhere in wiggly lines that threaten to dissolve. Their cries sound like excited birds. Their teachers, brisk and nervous, stride ahead and behind.

Down at the interpretive center, outside booths and tables are also filled with children. "Yuck," a little girl says judiciously, her hands covered with sticky clay. "Forget it," a boy grumbles as he fails to flint knap a stone into any semblance of a point. "This is hard," another child marvels, grinding kernels in a metate. Many of the children's cheeks and foreheads have been painted, crosses inside circles, suns, and eyes. Their faces are a heady mix, an American collage of black, white, and brown.

A popular booth is the atlatl throw. This long spear, set into a throwing stick, must be propelled vigorously straight from the shoulder. The goal is a cardboard figure reminiscent of a Christmas reindeer. A group of older boys are interested. "What happens when you hit the target?" one teenager asks the volunteer at the booth. "We say yea," the volunteer replies ironically. I watch a bearded stocky man take up the atlatl with unexpected assurance. He throws and misses the deer. "I was aiming for that turkey in the bushes," he jokes. He tries again, misses, and walks off muttering, "Something in the wrist, a snap of the wrist?" Next in line, a young girl gingerly picks up the atlatl. She poses for a moment, then collapses, giggling. Once again the Christmas deer is out of danger.

I think of my own son and daughter, who are not with me on this trip. I pause. But no, I don't miss them at all. For the moment I would rather watch children than be in charge of them.

Lighthearted, I take a walk through the park, a six-mile hike that winds deliriously through bluegrass and fescue, foxtail and timothy, panicum and paspalum, canary grass, barnyard grass, oatgrass, quackgrass, crabgrass, and a little bluestem. The rustles are from meadow vole and meadow jumping mice. The sounds I can distinguish are bobwhooit, teetiti, and keeeee: quail, lark, and hawk. I stand in the circle of large and imposing wood posts, the American version of Stonehenge, designed to herald the equinoxes. I am impressed by a replicated stretch of palisade, which originally required over 15,000 oak and hickory logs, each one twenty feet tall and a foot in diameter. I climb again to the top of Monks Mound. Who could resist? UNESCO was right. This is world class.

I also visit Mound 72, where a small plaque stands beside a grassy hump. All through the day, barely acknowledged, I have carried a prejudice against Cahokia. The rise of America's first urban landscape, that familiar tale of poverty and decay, is a little depressing. Moreover, I have known all along about this particular mound and its mass burials, mostly of women. In three separate pits were nineteen, twenty-two, and twenty-four sacrificed females. One burial of a forty-year-old male on a blanket of 20,000 marine shell beads required three women and three men, 800 arrowheads, fifteen chunkey stones, a pile of mica, and a roll of copper. In a nearby grave lay the skeletons of four men without heads or hands. In another deep pit were fifty-three strangled women, fifteen to twenty-five years old.

In the Cahokian belief of an afterlife, human sacrifice honored the dead and the sacrifices themselves. This custom was long-lived. When Hernando de Soto died in the New World in 1542, a local chief offered two men to be killed and buried with the Spanish conquistador. In 1725 at the death of a Natchez chief named Tattooed Serpent, two of his wives, a sister, his first warrior, his healer, his head speaker, his head speaker's wife, his nurse, and a man who made war clubs were also strangled. One of the wives had made friends with the French. She confided:

"Tattooed Serpent is in the country of the spirits, and in two days I will go to join him and will tell him that I have seen your heart shake at the sight of his dead body. Do not grieve. We will be friends for a much longer time in the country of the spirits than in this, because one does not die there again. It is always fine weather, one is never hungry, because nothing is wanting to live better than in this country. Men do not make war there anymore, because they make only one nation. I am going and leave my children without any father or mother. When you see them, Frenchmen, remember that you have loved their father and mother and that you ought not to repulse the children of the one who has always been the true friend of the French."

If her resignation is clear, any parent can also hear her pain. On top of Monks Mound I turned in a circle, and I knew why the Sun Kings wanted to build this high. I felt the intoxication of power. But in these fantasies of the past, I never really see myself as a king or a noble or even a rich merchant. I am always one of the women chosen to be sacrificed. I am the hapless wife of the head speaker. I grieve for what I'm leaving behind.

My walk does not end at Mound 72 but at one of the ponds near the museum. An eastern painted turtle moves slowly across the path. My seven-year-old son adores turtles, and I imagine his exclamation of pleasure and triumph. Suddenly I want him here, making sticky pots and chipping arrowheads, enjoying Kids Day at Cahokia Mounds State Park. Suddenly I am tired of traveling. I want to go home.

Sometime after the Civil War, in the last half of the nineteenth century, a Cherokee woman met a white man and started a lineage that eventually led to me and my son and daughter. That woman was my grandmother's great-grandmother. This is a very small drop of Mississippian blood. Even so, it means that certain of my ancestors may have lived among the Great Suns, whose job it was to keep the sacred fire, a bit of the real sun, burning in the temple on the mound. Some of my ancestors may have helped build those mounds. They tilled the cornfields. They knelt in reverence.

That thought makes me happy. I am like my son, filled with an irrational sense of accomplishment at the simple sight of a wild turtle. I have finally seen the great earthworks of Cahokia, and I have seen, as well, an eastern painted turtle, wet and unafraid. Intently he crawled across the path, flashing the vivid red markings on his neck, the lines of a secret map, the color of blood, the color of a sunset.

STEVE LEKSON IS WITTY. People do not generally laugh aloud while reading the reports produced by southwestern archaeologists. But when I am reading Steve, I occasionally do. Whatever rules bind his colleagues (no humor, no speculation, no figurative language, just the facts, ma'am, drowned in polysyllables or beaten to death by the whip end of a long sentence) do not bind him.

For example, in a paper called "Mimbres Art and Archaeology," he begins, "For two decades, I've hopped over most of the Southwest with one foot in my mouth; but my best errors—my personal favorites—were made in the Mimbres country."

The Mimbres country is where I live. While Cahokian priests climbed to the top of Monks Mound, village Mimbrenos (a subset of the Mogollons) were painting bowls with black and white designs so striking we still market them today. As Steve growls, "Mimbres motifs appear on an appalling range of kitchen utensils, knickknacks, clocks, souvenirs, handbags, T-shirts, fine clothing, neckties, Christmas ornaments, and corporate logos. You can't swing a cat in a Santa Fe gift shop without breaking a Mimbres-embellished tourist treasure."

"We find Mimbres art pleasing," Steve continues, "but Mimbres archaeology disappointing. A Mimbres site is a series of low, amorphous cobble mounds, pitted with hundreds of craters left behind by pot hunters. Mimbres ruins do not look like Mesa Verde ruins, Chaco Canyon ruins, or any of the other Ansel Adams/David Muench ruins. Anasazi is archetype for our Southwestern architectural aesthetic because Anasazi buildings look more like European (read "real") architecture (capital A) than do other Southwestern traditions." In effect the Mimbrenos are viewed as "artistic idiot savants who could paint a blue streak but could not stack three rocks up together."

Steve Lekson chides, "We think that the prehistoric societies with big pueblolike buildings or extensive canal irrigation were more developed (or better endowed or something) than those without. Pueblo-envy and canal-worship are an inextricable part of the milieu in which Southwestern archaeologists currently operate."

Pueblo-envy?

Well, Steve is a fine one to talk. He has spent a good part of his career at Chaco Canyon in northeastern New Mexico, arguably one of the best endowed ruins in this country. With its macho masonry work and drop-dead gorgeous scenery, Chaco Canyon is frankly a stud.

Like Cahokia, "downtown" Chaco covered about five square miles. The biggest ruin, Pueblo Bonito, was occupied from A.D. 900 to 1200 and contained over 600 rooms and 40 kivas (round rooms associated with cere-monial activity). The place is still massive, with four-story walls of sandstone block carefully coursed and tightly fit-ted. Visitors today walk through a maze of stone boxes, under T-shaped doorways, in a golden harmony of rock and sun. We feel strikingly glamorous in this Ansel Adams/David Muench photograph, where we have been chosen amazingly to serve as the model.

Other Great Houses, built during and after the tenth century, make Chaco a garden of ruins: Una Vida, 150 rooms and 5 kivas; Chetro Ketl, 500 rooms and 16 kivas; Pueblo del Arroyo, 280 rooms and 30 kivas; Kin Kletso, 100 rooms and 5 kivas. On North Mesa, Pueblo Alto stands at the junction of several prehistoric roads. On South Mesa, Tsin Kletzin commands the view. Below, Casa Rinconda is a sculpted flower of stone, the largest Great Kiva in the area. Casa Chiquita and Penasco Blanco are at the canyon's west end. Wijiji is to the east. Hundreds of smaller pueblos once defined the spaces in between.

"In A.D. 1000 a person looking out from Pueblo Bonito would have seen a built landscape," Steve Lekson says. "Almost everything in sight, save the canyon walls themselves, would have been built, shaped, or modified. The quantity and density of architecture was unprecedented. Rather than a canyon full of pueblos, Chaco was an integrated construct of substantial size."

The connections were made clear. Thirty-foot-wide walkways ran between the larger buildings. Terraces, shrines, signal stations, and platforms rimmed the canyon walls, with sloped ramps and staircases cut into the rock faces. The Chacoans also used platform mounds, mud walls, and other earthworks to create a public arena. Together, all the pueblos, kivas, mounds, ramps, plazas, pyres, walkways, shrines, votive boxes, and walls formed a ritual landscape with a complex "architectural vocabulary."

"The place is a theatre," Steve says. "It's meant to impress."

Unlike Cahokia, located on a major river and surrounded by fertile bottom land, Chaco is in a remote, rocky desert. Rainfall averages nine inches a year. The mesas and cliff walls are sparsely covered with patches of cactus and scrub brush. Temperatures range from 100 degrees Fahrenheit in the summer to 20 degrees below zero in the winter. With irrigation and run-off catchments, some agriculture was possible. But archaeologists debate how much. Almost every resource except for stone was scarce. The over 200,000 trees required to build the Great Houses had to be cut from forests nearly forty miles away. Environmentally, both the growth and decline of Cahokia make sense. The "Chaco Phenomenon" does not.

Then there are the roads, hundreds of miles of primitive highway that radiate from Chaco Canyon in every direction, over an area of 60,000 square miles. Some roads end at small settlements. Some lead to shrines. Some begin and end and go "nowhere." Some lead to outliers with their own Big Houses and Great Kivas.

The Great North Road is thirty feet wide and cleared to bedrock. It starts at Pueblo Alto, runs sixty miles to a wooden staircase at the head of a canyon, and follows the canyon floor to a large outlier we call Salmon Ruin. For a short section the road splits oddly into four parallel routes. In a Jemez Pueblo origin myth, a religious leader emerges from the underworld and makes four parallel paths by clearing away the brush. The four clans travel these paths separately and meet again on the way to Middle Place. Here is another potential for theatre, the large-scale reconstruction of myth. Like other Chaco roads, the North Road is marked by horseshoe-shaped shrines and broken pottery. This, too, suggests a modern Pueblo custom in which a pot containing the last meal of the dead is broken and scattered on a road leading north.

In 1972 Steve Lekson was part of a National Park Service team which found small interconnected storage rooms along the outside of Pueblo Alto. Although these rooms opened onto the roads, they were inaccessible from inside. The archaeologists also collected an extraordinary number of potsherds and estimated that in a sixty-year period more than 150,000 pots were discarded in one trash mound. The disposal of trash suggested a seasonal gathering of large groups. Like the other Great Houses, Pueblo Alto did not appear to have many permanent residents. Even the massive Pueblo Bonito may have been home to less than 100 people.

I am reminded of the Newark earthworks; Chaco Canyon also seems more ceremonial than urban, a place for pilgrims to congregate, worship, and be impressed. Trade, once again, may have been an important function, with Chaco the hub of a large regional network. Many miles away outliers show the same Chaco pattern of a central Great House, a nearby Great Kiva, small unit houses, and roadways entering the community. Steve Lekson thinks that this distinct architecture implies a common ideology, a shared sense of ritual among what may have been diverse populations. He suggests a level of social and political complexity not always granted the Anasazi.

"We haven't figured it out yet," Steve shrugs. "There's still a spectrum of opinion. There are still a lot of questions about social organization and hierarchy. Right now I think we can learn most from the outliers. What is their connection to Chaco? To each other? Like Chaco, certainly, they were built to last. Maybe that was part of the ideology. Maybe the people who lived there just didn't want to be bothered by upkeep. Maybe those buildings are a billboard. Maybe they mark turf.

"I see the roads as architecture. They are a clear connection between point A and point B. They say, 'We know who you are and where you live.' They also say, 'You have a direct route to the Emerald City.' I don't see armies marching up and down these roads, and I don't think they were necessary for trade. They were part of the larger ceremonial or political belief system."

In his paper on Mimbres art, Steve Lekson writes cheerfully that "the tentacles of the evil Chaco empire are stretching out over most of the piñon-juniper country, particularly within a 150-mile band centered roughly on the Continental Divide." He wonders if those tentacles did not reach all the way to me. A Mimbreno Great House and Kiva would not have been built of coursed sandstone, but of river cobble. They would look very different—and they would not last. Some archaeologists now believe they have found a road near the Old Town site in the Mimbres Valley with, yes, a nearby Great House and Kiva.

"Chaco on the Mimbres?" Steve concludes. "I do not expect to be believed and I do not exactly believe it myself. I have a long track record of being wrong about Mimbres culture. If I am right this time, I would like to be able to lean back in my rocker someday, knock over my tea, and say 'I told you so.' "

I smile at this image: an irascible Steve knocking over his tea. In the next scene he whacks me with his cane. Damn Interviewer. Feisty Old Archaeologist.

In fact Steve Lekson is about my age, in his early forties, a Research Fellow at the Crow Canyon Archaeological Center in Cortez, Colorado. Here, together, we sit and admire a view of the Mesa Verde Mountains. Crow Canyon combines research and education. They give a lot of tours, run a high school field school, work closely with Native Americans, teach teachers about archaeology, and direct a number of digs. Steve believes that this kind of non-profit organization, engaged with the public, outside the university and independent of the government, has an important role to play.

First, to be clear, Steve thinks archaeology is in trouble.

"Increasingly the field is divided between academic archaeology, with its insular and single scholar dynamic, and federally-mandated archaeology or Cultural Resource Management. For academics, sites are simply sources of data. For CRM archaeologists, employed by the National Park Service or the Forest Service or the BLM or some tribal group, sites are nonrenewable resources that must be conserved. Academics can be contemptuous of CRM. CRM can create regulations that pointedly restrict the research of academics. The antipathy is more than social. The two halves of archaeology reflect very different philosophies."

Steve also worries about the theory of archaeology, which he describes as "internally divided and intellectually paralyzed." Steve Lekson might be called a post–post-processualist.

"In the past we got away with a simple-minded materialism, and now there's a backlash. Beginning in the 1980s many archaeologists turned their backs on science and embraced a range of postmodern approaches taken from the humanities. By postmodern I mean a kind of postcolonial angst, a rejection of Western values. Postmodern archaeology couches questions in humanist terms that depend on aesthetics and personal experience. Archaeology has always had a foot in both camps, science and humanities, but now we seem to be backing away from science. Science is less important than people's feelings or their personal experience. I'm afraid that American archaeology may splinter, with half waltzing off into the humanities and the other half disappearing or shutting itself away from anthropology."

Finally, "American archaeology is under harsh criticism by the descendants of those it studies, particularly Native Americans, as a trivial discipline that adds little to social discourse at the cost of disturbed ancestral sites. Given the intellectual chaos and lack of direction in today's archaeology, it's difficult to answer this challenge with conviction. Native American critics may be right. Archaeology may be more trouble than it's worth."

Steve is playing the devil's advocate. He switches, quickly, to argue the other side.

"The world is full of surprises, but one is less surprised by them if you have an archaeological or anthropological background. The fact that people are beastly is not as surprising as the United Nations seems to think. Most of the institutions that shape our lives today—government, cities, economy, religion, ethnicity, war, peace—were invented and perfected long before written records. Many of the forces in our society began their trajectories in times known only to us through archaeology. I'm thinking of explosive population growth, human manipulation of the environment, the dynamic between people and technology. Archaeology gives us a scale that is much more realistic for thinking about things like Bosnia. People think they can make intelligent decisions based on history. But that's a pretty thin slice of time. What you are getting is how people work after writing, the tail end of things."

"Of course," Steve veers again, "maybe that is sufficient because we all think differently after writing. This kind of thinking may be so fixed that the other, earlier stuff is irrelevant. That's interesting, too."

This leads us to the notion of human nature, hardware versus software. We may still be using the Paleolithic brain, but we are running different programs. For instance, we read a lot. Does that kind of software have the ability to influence hardware? Did the Chacoans make a cognitive leap of software when they began to make architectural plans—foundations in the ground that served as one-to-one models—for the construction of buildings like Pueblo Bonito? And if these questions are important, if archaeology can help answer who we are now, then Steve asks, "Why has archaeology contributed almost nothing to current social and political thinking?"

He returns to his first point. Archaeology is in trouble, and archaeology needs to change. He sees a disciplinary revolution and a cross-disciplinary infusion of ideas. The first step would be to bring people together, "leaders in every facet of archaeology, Native peoples, public educators, economists, market analysts, futurists and social scientists, philosophers and policy makers. Most importantly we need to find the people and institutions whose goals and missions are change, who have made the study and analysis of change their strength."

We segue into Steve's flirtation with complexity theory, which looks at the variables of complex systems and seeks to find any underlying rules. I hear the echo of New Archaeology, that can-do attitude, science as oracle. But complexity theory does not underestimate its task. A popular image of complex systems is that of a butterfly flapping its wings in Brazil and causing a rainstorm over London. Highly variable systems such as weather may be virtually unknowable. Still, the scientists of complexity are trying. They believe, for example, that evolving systems like human societies adapt and learn best at the border between order and chaos. Steve hopes the way these societies "self-organize" can be discovered.

With less restraint than usual he talks about these ideas when he compares Chaco and Cahokia. Both peaked and crashed between A.D. 900 and 1200. Both, Steve writes "were monumental on a scale that surpassed anything before or after; both crystallized more modest preceding traditions and shaped the trajectories of all that followed. . . . Chaco and Cahokia—coincidence? As

Jack Palance used to hiss: believe it or not. I'd prefer to believe that the parallels between Chaco and Cahokia are telling us something. I submit that Chaco and Cahokia represent examples of spontaneous self-organization, independent of each other but operating in the same dimensional space."

Archaeology and complexity theory. As Jack Palance used to hiss: Why not? Chaco and Cahokia were confabulations of myth and mortar, the living shape of a dream. They deserve the scrutiny of visionaries.

Out of chaos comes order. Steve Lekson became an archaeologist because "it combined brain work with outside work." Also, he visited Pompei, Italy, as a kid. Then in his first year at college, someone told him he had to declare a major. Archaeology was in the A's. Somewhere a butterfly flapped its wings.

At the Crow Canyon Archaeological Center, we sit on wooden steps and enjoy the sun's last heat of the day. I have spent the morning at Chaco Canyon and am glowing still from its beauty and light. Steve broods on the prospect of disciplinary revolution—together in one room, futurists and physicists, politicians and archaeologists. Those kinds of meetings and intellectual shifts require funding. They lack, at the moment, a certain specifity.

"We may actually do some of these things and, in fact, transform North American archaeology," Steve Lekson says. Then he turns and reconsiders, metaphorically knocking over his tea. "On the other hand, we might do nothing at all and archaeology will plod along, quite the same."

FIRST CONTACT

HISTORIANS KNOW OF OVER EIGHTY VOYAGES from Europe to the New World between 1492 and 1504. Most ships explored south and west of the Caribbean Islands. But as the natives there died of flu, smallpox, and other diseases, slave raids throughout the area became common. Slaves were also shipped from Africa, introducing new plagues like malaria, typhoid, typhus, and yaws. In 1512 Juan Ponce de León discovered what he called La Florida for the *flores,* or "flowers," of that Easter season. In 1519 Álvarez de Pineda explored the Gulf coastline of Florida and realized this was not just another island. In 1521 Ponce de León returned with cows, pigs, horses, and sheep; he later died in a battle with Native Americans. In 1526, 600 settlers lived for three months on the coast of Georgia before they fled, leaving behind their escaped African slaves.

In 1528 Panfilo de Narváez, described by his own contemporaries as greedy and incompetent, tried his hand at conquering the land named for flowers. Near Tampa Bay Governor Narváez sent his ships north while he, 300 men, and forty horses marched into the interior. Eight years later, four survivors of the expedition—accompanied by hundreds of Indian followers—met up with Spanish slave hunters in north-central Mexico. For most of their exile, Álvar Núñez Cabeza de Vaca, Alonso del Castillo, Andres Dorantes, and the Moor Estaban had been held captive by coastal Indians. More recently, they had walked across Texas and Mexico healing the sick and raising the dead. This extraordinary story was published in 1542 as *La Relación,* Cabeza de Vaca's final report to the king of Spain. It sells in bookstores even today.

Amid some fish nets we found a gold rattle.

From the beginning Governor Narváez was after one particular metal. The gold rattle had been discovered early, stolen from a small village near Tampa Bay. Soon after, the Spanish captured four Timucuans who told them more gold could be found north in a province called Apalachen. In a third encounter with the natives, on the other side of the Withlacoochee River, *about 200 Indians moved toward us. The Governor went to meet them and talked in signs. They gestured so menacingly that we fell upon them and seized five or six, who led us to their houses half a league away. There we found quite a quantity of corn ripe for plucking.*

Pressing forward, using the captive Indians as guides, the soldiers soon saw an astonishing sight, *a chief in a painted deerskin riding the back of another Indian, musicians playing reed flutes walking before, and a train of many subjects attending him. He dismounted where the Governor stood and stayed an hour. We apprised him by signs that we were on our way to Apalachen. His signs seemed to mean that he was an enemy of the Apalachee and would accompany us against them. We gave him beads, little bells, and other trinkets, and he gave the Governor the deerskin he wore. When he turned back, we followed.*

The next day over 300 Spanish soldiers ate corn at the chief's home. In the night the Timucuans crept away and later attacked the foreigners on the trail. Again the Governor captured guides who took the men—through forests of trees that were astonishingly high—to an Apalachen village on the Aucilla River. The village contained only women and children in small, thatched houses sheltered from the frequent storms. The soldiers found a large stand of corn ready to pick, as well as other dried food, deerskins, and shawls woven of thread.

Typically, *two hours after we arrived in Apalachen, the Indians who had fled returned in peace to ask for the release of their women and children. We released them. The Governor, however, continued to hold one of their chiefs, upon which they grew agitated and attacked us the next day.*

So it went. The Spanish stole food and kidnapped people. The fierce, well-organized Apalachee fought back. For a month Governor Narváez stayed in the area while his "guides" whispered of a prosperous settlement to the south, close to the sea and full of food. But when the army marched there, they found only a deserted village, its houses burned. Daily, things became more desperate. Cabeza de Vaca returned from a scouting trip to find the Governor and many others so sick that *the men could not move, most of them lying prone and those able to stand duty very few.* Next the soldiers in the calvary plotted to desert, but were fortunately dissuaded.

A third of our force had fallen seriously ill and was growing worse by the hour. We felt certain we would all be stricken, with death the one foreseeable way out; and in such a place, death seemed all the more terrible. Considering our experiences, our prospects, and various plans, we finally concluded to undertake the formidable project of constructing vessels to float away in. This appeared impossible, since none of us knew how to build ships, and we had no tools, iron, forge, oakum, pitch, or rigging, or any of the indispensable items, or anybody to instruct us. Worse still, we had no food to sustain workers. At this impasse, we agreed to consider the matter deeper and ended our parley for the day, each going his way, commending our future to God our Lord.

Over 450 years later I also commend myself to God, get on an airplane, and fly to Tampa to follow the route of the incompetent and greedy Panfilo de Narváez. A number of tourists in Florida have been recently murdered, and the car rental office is ominous with signs that read, "Lock your doors!" Feeling timid, I drive through a long strip of fast-food America. Within hours the Withlacoochee River is a shiny snake out my window.

At the Manatee Springs State Park, I stop and eat lunch. Nearby *one of the mounted men, Juan Velasquez, impatiently rode into the river. The violent current swept him from his saddle. He grabbed the reins but drowned with the horse.* Today Cabeza de Vaca would still recognize these *immense trees and open woods containing nut varieties, laurels, a species called liquid amber, cedars, junipers, live-oaks, pines, red-oaks, and low palmettos like those of Castille.* Idling down a trail, I see a blob in the water that a woman behind me identifies as a manatee. This same woman croons to her cranky granddaughter, "Way down upon the Suwannee River, far far from home," and I am startled to realize that this is the famous Southern river I sang about so often in my grade school music class. The scene is a postcard with groves of muscular cypress and tall sweet gum draped in moss. (The song, unfortunately, takes hold like a leech and I will find myself humming, unwillingly, at any moment, "that's where the old folks staaaay.")

In Tallahassee I find and take as my captive guide Rochelle Marrinan from Florida State University. We meet east of the city at Patale, the site of a 1633 Spanish mission. These are wealthy suburbs, and Patale is in the front yard of a country mansion whose owners have hosted a field school dig every winter for eleven years.

Field work at Patale is also a university class. Nine graduate students and thirteen undergraduates move in and out of two irregularly shaped holes, about ten feet across and two feet deep, cut carefully from the green lawn. At the end of the semester, the students will get grades, the holes will be covered with sod, and Rochelle will know more about this mission and about missions in general.

Now she wonders why what she thinks is the kitchen was placed so close to the church. We step into the "church" and look for the altar. Sixty-seven Apalachees were buried here under the floor. The orientation of their heads is important. "There was a tradition of clergy buried facing the congregation and of communicants buried facing the altar," Rochelle says. "In the afterlife these Apalachee would have been able to sit up, looking southwest, and see the altar immediately." She points out discolorations in the ground, subtle patterns that show where a post hole once stood. Her trowel appears magically, an archaeologist's trick. "No, see, but this is from a rodent," she murmurs, scraping at a yellow patch.

I am kidnapping Rochelle for the afternoon, leaving her graduate assistant in charge. Briefly we pause to look at the view of rolling horse pasture, with scattered houses amid clumps of live oak and pine. In 1528 those pastures would have been cornfields and those houses made of thatch amid clumps of large oak, hickory, and magnolia. It would not have looked so very different.

As we go, Rochelle's assistant calls out, "Don't let the gators get you!"

My heart leaps.

"Yeah, you'll see plenty of alligators," Rochelle assures me as we drive to the St Marks Wildlife Refuge, where Narváez and his men fell ill and built their barges. "You'll be bored with alligators before we're through."

Rochelle loves the story of Cabeza de Vaca. She empathizes. "Imagine their fears, to die here alone, to never again see the people you know and love, to die unacknowledged and without the sacraments, completely separated from your culture. Cabeza de Vaca was older, about forty, but most of these men were young men. They thought they were invulnerable."

For Rochelle, different cultures and different pasts have compelled her ever since she was a little girl picking up artifacts in Florida orange groves. Her mother wanted her to become a nurse. "You can always do something else," her mother said sensibly, "if you don't like it." So Rochelle became a nurse, and then she became an archaeologist.

As we pass through Tallahassee, we talk of shell mounds, epidemics, AIDS, science fiction, poverty, social reform. First contact is a powerful prism. This is the beginning of modern America. One archaeologist has suggested we can only see this time from the cubists' perspective: multiple, simultaneous views of the same subject, "an infinite number of momentary glimpses."

At the St Marks Wildlife Refuge we walk to where a fire tower stands on a burial mound. Excavated in the 1930s, the grave goods here included Clarksdale bells and Nueva Cadiz beads, Spanish products dating from the first half of the sixteenth century. Rochelle announces quietly, "This is the best candidate for a Narváez-related site."

Somewhere in this bay the Governor and his men turned sweet gum resin into calk and pine pitch into tar. One of the soldiers fashioned wooden pipes and deerskin bellows so they could melt their metal equipment to forge nails, axes, and other tools. From palmetto husks and horsetails, they braided ropes and rigging; from their shirts, they sewed sails; from flayed horses' skins, they made water bottles. They also raided nearby Apalachee villages and *in spite of armed resistance, netted as much as one hundred bushels of corn*. Still, by the time the Spanish sailed, they had lost forty men from disease and hunger, in addition to those killed by Indians.

Rochelle prowls and spots some pottery sherds near my feet. "Deptford," she says, "pre-1500s."

We drive on through the marshy refuge, past canals and inlets. Egrets fly up startlingly white. Ibises stalk the green sedge. At the St Marks lighthouse, land concedes gracefully to water. With the gulf shore on one side and a canal on the other, I see red-winged blackbirds, wood ducks, blue herons, a kingfisher, a cardinal. To the north trees rise above the spiky palmettos. To the south a turquoise sea is darkened by reefs and hidden oyster beds. I pine for an alligator.

"Ah, there he is," Rochelle whispers.

The fifteen-foot animal basks some twenty feet away, on the other side of the canal. A cliché with yellow eyes that blink balefully, the reptile looks surprisingly fake, rubbery, kickable. When we move closer, however, the gator slips quickly into the water. The next day, returning to the refuge, I will see a dozen more. I never get bored.

"Poor guys," Rochelle says, referring to Panfilo de Narváez and his men. She motions to the dangerous shallow reefs, the palmetto-spiked land, the brittle marsh grass like a thousand small knives. "This was such tough country, marshy, scratchy, hostile. They had a rough time here. Finally they left Florida. It didn't get better."

Indeed, after thirty days adrift in the Gulf of Mexico, *our thirst was killing us; the salt water was killing us.* When the barges landed near Pensacola, they were attacked by Indians and not one of the men escaped injury. At Mobile Bay the Spanish skirmished again with local tribes. At the Mississippi River the boats lost sight of each other. Cabeza de Vaca at last saw Narváez's ship which *having the healthiest and strongest men was making quickly for land. Now I yelled to him to throw me a rope so we could stay with him.* But Narváez refuses, saying only *that each must do as he thought best to save himself; that this was what he was doing now.* With these words Governor Narváez disappeared from history.

Abandoned, near death, Cabeza de Vaca and his crew landed near Galveston Island, where friendly Capoque Indians brought them fish and roots. In an attempt to embark, two of the men drowned and the barges capsized. *The Indians, understanding our full plight, sat down and lamented for half an hour, so loudly they could have been heard a long way off. It was amazing to see these wild, untaught savages howling like brutes in compassion for us.* Moreover, the natives saved the starving, unclothed Spanish by taking them to their village, *supporting us under their arms, they hurried us from one to another of the four big fires they had built along the path. At each fire, when we regained a little warmth and strength, they took us on so swiftly our feet hardly touched the ground.*

This era of good feeling would soon end.

Five Christians quartered on the coast came to the extremity of eating each other . . . and the Indians were so shocked at this cannibalism that, if they had seen it sometime earlier, they surely would have killed every one of us. Then half the natives died from a disease of the bowels and blamed us.

From now on the Spanish survivors would be treated as slaves. Most of the time they went hungry, for these tribes lived painfully close to the margin. *Three months out of every year they eat nothing but oysters and drink very bad water. Wood is scarce; mosquitos plentiful.* Sometimes the castaways were elevated to the position of shamans. *Our method was to bless the sick, breathe upon them, recite a Pater noster and Ave maria, and pray earnestly to God our Lord for their recovery.*

Then, inexplicably, things would go wrong again. *My life became unbearable. In addition to much other work, I had to grub roots in the water or from underground in the canebrakes. My fingers got so raw that if a straw touched them they would bleed.*

After one year, Cabeza de Vaca found a way to move up the social ladder. He escaped from the Capoques and became a trader. *My principal wares were cones and other pieces of seashell, conches used for cutting, sea-beads, and a fruit like a bean which the Indians value highly, using it for medicine and for a ritual beverage in their dances and festivities. This is the sort of thing I carried inland. By barter I got and brought back to the coast skins, red ocher which they rub on their faces, hard canes for arrows, flint for arrowheads, with sinews and cement to attach them, and tassels of deer hair which they dye red. This occupa-*

tion suited me; I could travel where I wished, was not obliged to work and was not a slave.

Time passed. Cabeza de Vaca writes, *I was in the region for nearly six years.* He then skips quickly over these years. Did he take a wife? Father children? If so, the former gentleman does not report this to the king of Spain. Not all adventures can be told. Instead, *La Relación* provided its royal reader with pages of anthropological description. This was Europe's first detailed look at North America. Cabeza de Vaca proved to be an exceptional observer.

The Capoques and Hans *are tall and well-built. Their only weapons are bow and arrows, which they use with great dexterity. The men bore through one of their nipples, some both, and insert a joint of cane two and a half palms long by two fingers thick. They also bore their lower lip and wear a piece of cane in it half a finger in diameter. . . .*

Their women toil incessantly. From October to the end of February every year, which is the season these Indians live on the island, they subsist on the roots I have mentioned, which the women get from under water in November and December. Only in these two months, too, do they take fish in their cane weirs. When the fish is consumed, the roots furnish the only staple. At the end of February the islanders go into other parts to seek sustenance for then the root is beginning to grow and is not edible.

These people love their offspring more than any in the world and treat them very mildly.

By contrast, further west, the Quevenes were more cruel and consistently kicked and beat their Spanish slaves. Unpleasantly, they and the Mariames *take life, destroying even their male children, on account of dreams. They cast away their daughters at birth; the dogs eat them. They say they do this because all the nations of the region are their enemies, with whom they war ceaselessly; and that if they were to marry off their daughters, the daughters would multiply their enemies until the latter overcame and enslaved the Mariames, who thus preferred to annihilate all daughters than risk their reproduction of a single enemy. . . . This is also the practice of their neighbors, the Yguaces, but of no other people of that region. . . .*

To marry, men buy wives from their enemies, the price of a wife being the best bow that can be got. . . . A marriage lasts no longer than suits the parties; they separate on the slightest pretext. . . .

The men bear no burdens. Anything of weight is borne by women and old men, the people least esteemed. They do not love their children as do the Capoques.

Even so the harsh Mariames and Yguaces *are a merry people, considering the hunger they suffer. They never skip their fiestas and areitos. To them the happiest time of the year is the season of eating prickly pears. They go in no want then and pass the whole time dancing and eating, day and night.*

Elsewhere in his report Cabeza de Vaca discusses homosexuality, eunuchs, birth control, weaning, and the making of peyote tea. He explains methods of battle and the usefulness of women as negotiators, commenting that *All these tribes are warlike and have as much strategy for protection against enemies as if they had been reared in Italy in continuous feuds.*

At some point the trader was reduced again to slavery. In different seasons, gathering prickly pears or nuts, he reunited with the few remaining Spanish and learned how all five barges had been lost and how each hidalgo had met his death. Finally in the fall of 1534, the last four Christians made a united escape. Do or die, they prepared to walk to Mexico, into the sun.

The miracles began.

Reviving their roles as shamans, the Spanish passed from tribe to tribe curing headaches, cramps, and other ills. Early on, in one dramatic case, *I saw that the man we hoped to save was dead: many mourners were already weeping around him, and his house was already down, sure signs that the inhabitant was no more. I found his eyes rolled up, his pulse gone, and every appearance of death, as Dorantes agreed. Taking off the mat that covered him, I supplicated our Lord in his behalf and in behalf of the rest who ailed, as fervently as I could. After my blessing and breathing on him many times, they brought me his bow and a basket of pounded prickly pears.*

The natives then took me to treat many others who had fallen into a stupor and gave me two more baskets of prickly pears. I in turn gave these to the Indians who accompanied us. We returned to our lodgings while the Indians whom we had given the fruit waited till evening to return.

When they got back that evening, they brought the tidings that the "dead" man I had treated had got up whole and walked; he had eaten and spoken with these Indians who further reported that all I had ministered to had recovered and were glad. Throughout the land the effect was a profound wonder and fear. People talked of nothing else and wherever the fame of it reached, people set out to find us so we should cure them and bless their children.

In the rugged hill country of Texas, the Spanish still suffered. Among the Avavares and Ardobaos they endured acute hunger. Also, in the desert, *The sun and air raised great painful sores on our chests and shoulders and our heavy loads caused the cords to cut our arms. The region is so broken and so overgrown that often, when we gathered wood, blood flowed from us in many places where the thorns and shrubs tore our flesh.*

As the four healers moved west, into more prosperous country, they became surrounded by a growing number of attendants. *Those who accompanied us plundered our hospitable new hosts and ransacked their huts, leaving nothing. We watched this with deep concern but were in no position to do anything about it so for the present had to bear with it until such time as we might gain greater authority. Those who had lost their possessions, seeing our dejection, tried to console us. They said they were so honored to have us that their property was well bestowed—and that they would get repaid by others farther on, who were very rich.*

This was a kind of pyramid scheme.

One village, caught unprepared, *lost all they had and shed copious tears. Their plunderers told them that we were children of the sun with power to save or destroy, along with even bigger lies, which none can tell better than they. They cautioned our hosts to avoid offending us in any way, to give us all they had left, and to take us to a populous village, which custom privileged them to plunder. Then the plunderers went back.*

Rolena Adorno, a professor of Romance languages at Princeton University, believes that Cabeza de Vaca's success depended on these patterns of ritual exchange.

The "miracles" occurred when established forms of intertribal behavior, traditional healing practices, and devout Catholicism miraculously combined. The natives perceived, for their own purposes, the Spanish to be powerful shamans, and shamans they became. By and large the Christians hardly seemed to be in control of the situation.

They ever plundered each other and those who lost were as content as those who gained. We attracted more followers than we could manage or employ. . . . Every Indian brought his portion to us to be breathed on and blessed before he would dare touch it. When you consider that we were frequently accompanied by three or four thousand Indians and were obliged to sanctify the food and drink of each one, as well as grant permission for the many things they asked to do, you can appreciate our inconvenience.

Somewhere below El Paso, Texas, this medicine man, revival, and traveling show entered a well-populated area of Pima Indians. *Among this people, women are better treated than in any part of the Indes we had come through. They wear knee-length cotton skirts and, over them, half-sleeved shirts of scraped deerskin that reach to the ground and that are laced together in front with leather strips. The women soap this outer garment with a certain root which cleanses and keeps the deerskin becoming. And they wear shoes.*

On their part the healers had become increasingly austere.

We Christians traveled all day without food, eating only at night—and then so little as to astonish our escort. We never felt tired, being so inured to hardship, which increased our enormous influence. . . . Through all these nations, the people who were

at war quickly made up so they could come meet us with every-
thing they possessed. Thus we left all the land in peace. And we
taught all the people by signs, which they understood, that in
Heaven was a Man we called God, who had created the heavens
and earth; that all good came from Him and that we worshipped
and obeyed Him and called him our Lord; and that if they would
so the same, all would be well with them.

More and more, Cabeza de Vaca was seeing signs of
his countrymen—slave traders who had passed through
the area. On one hand, he rejoiced. On the other, *We told*
the natives we were going after those men to order them to stop
killing, enslaving, and dispossessing the Indians; which made
our friends very glad.

At last the four companions and their followers met
an escort of Spanish calvary. After general amazement and
celebration, the captain of the company attempted to take
the loyal Pimas as slaves.

Alcaraz bade his interpreter tell the Indians that we were
members of his race which had been long lost; that his group were
the lords of the land who must be obeyed and served, while we
were inconsequential. The Indians paid no attention to this.
Conferring among themselves, they replied that the Christians
lied: We had come from the sunrise, they came from the sunset;
we healed the sick, they killed the sound; we came naked and
barefoot, they clothed, horsed, and lanced; we coveted nothing
but gave whatever we were given, while they robbed whomever
they found and bestowed nothing on anyone.

Chagrined, Captain Alcaraz arrested Cabeza de Vaca
and his friends and sent them away *in the charge of an alcade*
named Cebreros, attended by two horsemen. They took us

*through forests and wastes so we would not communicate with
the natives and would neither see nor learn of their crafty scheme
afoot.* Meanwhile, the captain stayed behind to capture the
unfortunate remaining Indians.

Years later in his report to the king, Cabeza de Vaca
stood staunchly by his last transforming conclusion,
*Clearly, to bring all these people to Christianity and subjection
to Your Imperial Majesty, they must be won by kindness, the
only certain way.*

Throughout the sixteenth century the Spanish
would debate their treatment of natives in the New
World. Cabeza de Vaca's account was published twice
during the reign of Charles V and read avidly by reform-
ers like Bartolomé de las Casas, who helped change the
legal status of Indians under Spanish rule.

"The success of Cabeza de Vaca's writing," Rolena
Adorno says, "can be explained by the fact that it took a
counter-conquest position. That is, Cabeza de Vaca advo-
cated peaceful conversion of the natives and demonstrated
that good treatment of the Indians produced results that
served both the well-being of native populations and the
economic interests of the Spanish."

In the end men like Bartolomé de las Casas only
blunted the Spanish sword. They could not prevent the
widespread enslavement of Native Americans.

After returning to Spain Cabeza de Vaca sailed to
South America, where he commanded two more overland
expeditions. On these he prohibited his soldiers from looting, raping, and exploiting local tribes. Political intrigue
prevented further reform. Eventually Cabeza de Vaca's

own men sent him home in chains. Back in Spain he was banished for eight years to Africa. During this time his wife spent her fortune to gain him a pardon. She was successful. In 1556 Charles V named Cabeza de Vaca Chief Justice of the Tribunal of Seville. The former conquistador died a few years later. One could say he had lived a full life.

AT THE MUSEUM OF NATURAL HISTORY in Gaines-ville, Florida, under a dim light, on a long table, Kathleen Deagan spreads out her Spanish treasure: small brass bells, tiny silver beads, fragments of Green Bacin pottery, an iron chisel, a few nails, three interlocking brass rings.

Lightly, with a gloved hand, she touches an incised copper pendant. "Oh, I haven't seen this in ages," she says.

I, too, am wearing white cotton gloves that will prevent my skin oil from altering the composition of five-hundred-year-old metal. The artifacts here have just returned from a traveling exhibit and are ready to be stored again in this safe, dark, temperature-controlled underground, behind locked doors and signs that say "No Entrance, Security, Personnel Only"—the shivery bowels of the Florida Museum of Natural History.

Admittedly I am dramatizing. Still, there is something glamorous and secretive about this scene. In this room I have discovered a subset of archaeological passion: curation.

Kathleen shows me the museum's new storage system. Jammed closely together these rows of floor-to-ceiling metal containers are twenty feet long, with mechanical tracks that allow only one access aisle to appear at a time. "We've nearly doubled our space," Kathleen says with pleasure. We set the tracks to moving—clang, clank—and walk through a newly opened passage to a drawer marked with the right number. Inside are Cadiz Nueva beads from the burial mound Rochelle and I visited at the St Marks Wildlife Refuge. The oblong shapes of colored glass are reminiscent of the 1960s, when hippie stores sold similar striped beads in combinations of white, red, blue, and black. The drawer also contains a Clarksdale bell, bits of clay ollas, a Civil War button, a broken bottle, and other odds and ends, all carefully wrapped, numbered, catalogued, saved, and valued.

Kathleen Deagan has been excavating Spanish colonial sites for over twenty years. On the island of Hispaniola she directs work at Isabella, the luckless town founded by Christopher Columbus in 1494. In Florida her long-term projects include the Spanish Plymouth Rock, a 1565 fort near Saint Augustine.

Historical archaeology is the study of sites created in the Americas within the last five hundred years, what some call the Modern Period. The field is tremendously complex, with its own ferment of theoretical dispute and controversy.

"We use the combined avenues of material analysis and documentary analysis," Kathleen says. "Sometimes we have access to an almost overwhelming documentary base. But in the story of first contact, especially, if you just deal with documents, you only have one side of the story.

Historical archaeology gives a voice to people who don't usually have a voice. That is true even when we are dealing with literate people. If you are poor or female or illiterate or an ethnic minority, you don't always appear in the historical record. A lot of historical archaeology is now being done in urban sites, and we're getting a much less one dimensional view of places like colonial Boston or nineteenth-century Phoenix."

Kathleen talks about Fort Mose, a 1738 colony established in northern Florida by escaped slaves from British Carolina. The Spanish freed these slaves in exchange for military service. Like other Black Militia, the men and women at Fort Mose fought in a number of important battles against the English.

"We had always known about Fort Mose, but we didn't know where it was," Kathleen says. "Then the Black Caucus here in Florida funded a search for the site. After five years of excavation and research, we now have a traveling exhibit that has been very well received by the African-American community. It shows the resistance of black people, their refusal to stay slaves. This kind of archaeology can make a difference to people who are still disenfranchised."

Most of Kathleen's work, however, is 200 years before Fort Mose, on the skittering edge of first contact. "The thing that interests me is the concept of an integrated hybrid-American society that's part European, part African, part Native American. Every society is an amalgamation. Usually we see the end product. Here in the New World we can look at the beginning, raw and happening. This is the study and process of encounter, of acculturation and adaptive changes, the nature of the European imposition, the outcome of all that! What happened then had profound consequences for where we are now. In Latin America, especially, you can see how much Indian women shaped the domestic life of the Spanish colonists. I think these women had a tremendous role as culture brokers in the formation of a new society."

Like Rochelle Marrinan and others who work on Spanish sites, Kathleen dismisses the idea that Spanish colonists were particularly cruel. "Yes, the Black Legend." She makes a face. "I see very little difference between how the Spanish and other Europeans treated Native Americans. In some ways Anglo treatment was harsher. Looking at an Anglo site, you wouldn't dream that an Indian was anywhere around. But in Spanish sites you see a true melting pot. There was a lot of intermarriage. Native American women were very much present in things like how food was processed and what foods were eaten. There was a difference in the African experience too. Again, Anglo sites were more highly segregated. I think the 700-year occupation of Spain by the Moors accustomed the Spanish to a greater mix of cultures."

However you mix them, for most Native Americans, first contact was a death sentence. "The disease vectors came early," Kathleen agrees. "In the first year at Isabella, in 1494, half the Europeans and half the Indians both died at the same rate, probably from equine or swine flu. The African slaves brought their diseases. The

Europeans brought their diseases. By 1528, when Cabeza de Vaca got here, there had been plenty of opportunities to infect Florida. It's interesting, though, that Florida sustained big Indian populations up until the eighteenth century. It may have been these very early epidemics that helped immunize the population. Then when the English came, there was a series of raids, and thousands of Indians were killed. The rest were congregated in missions like St. Augustine, where they were vulnerable to new epidemics."

Until recently depopulation has been a numbers game. Archaeologists argued that in 1491 the New World had 13 million people, no, 30 million people, no, 100 million people. We do know that in some areas Native Americans declined by as much as 95 percent within five to six generations after European contact. In the United States a population of 12 million (a high estimate) might have dropped to 600,000.

"There's little archaeological evidence of depopulation, no huge graveyards," Kathleen Deagan says. "But in the written accounts from the Spanish and the French, we get their horror and alarm at what is happening. Their projections of death rates are even higher than what archaeologists say today. I tend to agree with the larger numbers."

A few people are now exploring the emotional content of these numbers. Two or three diseases often attacked a tribe at once, with the complete loss of vulnerable age groups like the young and old. There was a whipsaw effect on fertility, on hope, on the future. Normal patterns of social life collapsed. Victims were too weak to get food and water. Relatives fled in terror. Prayer meant nothing. One archaeologist writes, "In the tumultuous environment of agonizing mass death, despair may well have been, in the end, the most destructive force of all."

First contact was a holocaust, and Americans walk on the bones of millions who died in unspeakable grief. I ask Kathleen Deagan what I also asked Rochelle Marrinan. Isn't their field somewhat grim?

"Oh, yes, it's grim," Rochelle says.

"Very grim," Kathleen says.

"But there's more than just that," she goes on. "There has also been strength and survival, maybe not in the original form, but it's there. Latin America today is no less Indian than it is European. To say that Indians are extinct there is like saying Europeans are extinct. Even in Florida, if the Spanish hadn't evacuated the last remaining Timucuans, there would be Florida Indians here. I have the underlying belief that nothing ever stays in the same form. It can't. Archaeology drills into us that change is the one inevitable stable thing in the world. Evolution is going to happen. Maybe it's from the inside. Maybe it's from the outside."

In the currents of conversation we wind these threads back and forth, picking up other threads. "There's a modern emphasis in archaeology, in postprocessualism, of many voices, of many different perspectives," Kathleen Deagan says, "that's part of the older issue of cultural relativism, that there are many cultural ways of looking at the same thing and one is not necessarily better than the other. But the world is global now. Today you really can't understand anything from your own cultural context alone. There are so few cultural contexts that are not connected to other cultural contexts and, through them, to all other cultural contexts. Everything is interconnected."

I hold a Nueva Cadiz bead in my hand, perhaps a bead that the greedy Governor Narváez once gave an Apalachen chief. Soon I will be on a plane thousands of feet in the air. These two things are not unrelated. First contact. The two halves of the world met, and we became one world. What Japanese businessmen do today influences what I do tomorrow. The health of Africa has become my health. The future of America is tied to the well-being of all its people, even to those who just crossed our border—waded the river or stepped off a boat. We are still in the process of encounter, acculturation, and adaptive change.

It is no wonder we walk into a bookstore, buy a translation of *La Relación,* and read Cabeza de Vaca with interest and familiarity. Yes, we think, that's the adventure we are on.

A GOOD WISH

ROGER ECHO-HAWK, A TRIBAL HISTORIAN FOR the Pawnee of Oklahoma, lectures to a class of aspiring archaeologists, museum directors, and curators. It is not, really, a lecture. Roger prefers to tell a story, with a plot and subplots that nicely intertwine.

He begins with Thomas Jefferson, "the father of American archaeology," who pioneered scientific methods in the excavation of an Indian mound on his Virginia plantation. "Although he knew this was a burial site," Roger says, "there is no evidence that Jefferson sought to consult with any local Indians. In that, he set a precedent."

Meanwhile in New York, medical students were stealing bodies for dissection from black and poor cemeteries. "These issues are complex." Roger's voice is smooth, measured, and calm. "Let's say there are two doctors. One believes it is unethical to secretly exhume and use people like this. The other doctor believes it's okay. They both work in a hospital. One day you go in with a bullet somewhere in your chest or stomach. Which doctor would you want to operate? I know which one I would want. I'd want the one who had the most experience opening up bodies."

Apparently New Yorkers felt the same way—until the students began digging in the city's more prosperous white graveyards. A scandal followed, and public riots led to the 1790 Anatomy Acts which regulated what could be done to the dead.

Roger Echo-Hawk stands comfortably before the class, his long black hair tied back in a ponytail. He spreads his hands, palms up. "The people of America said clearly, 'We won't let science go unrestrained in the graves of our citizens.' But there were no riots in Virginia. No one cared about Indian burials. That was the beginning of a double standard."

At about this time on the plains of Nebraska, the son of a prominent Skidi Pawnee was born. Man Chief or Pitarisaru grew up to be a leader both Pawnee and Americans could admire. In the early nineteenth century the Pawnee were especially interested in trade, and in 1821 they sent Man Chief to Washington, D.C., where he made a strong impression. James Fenimore Cooper wrote of the chief's "grave and haughty, though still courteous mien, the restless but often steady, and bold glance of his dark, keen eye, and the quiet dignity of his air." Fictionalized in Cooper's novels, Man Chief became part of a young nation's literature. In Philadelphia a women's school presented him with a silver medal. To the Pawnee such medallions signified the right of their leaders to conduct international relations. When Man Chief died a few years later, he was buried with his medal in his homeland. In another fifty years the Pawnees would be relocated to Oklahoma, leaving Man Chief's grave behind.

In the mid-1800s Dr. Samuel Morton, "the father of physical anthropology," was using cranial measurements to rank racial groups in terms of superiority and intelligence. The call went out: scientists needed Indian skulls. Eventually Dr. Morton's theories were rejected. But the collection of Native American bones continued. In 1868 the U.S. Surgeon General ordered its personnel to submit Indian craniums to the Army Medical Museum. This was done, in part, so that physicians could study the prevention and care of head wounds. Army doctors dutifully sent in thousands of remains from battlefields and burial grounds. Natural history museums also wanted Indian material, as curators hurried to preserve cultures they believed were doomed to extinction.

"In the minds of these people, there were compelling reasons to dig up these burials," Roger says without sarcasm, and I am struck by his deliberate sense of fair play. In his discussions of history, in his work with both races, Roger chooses neither to demonize nor idealize.

This reasonable position is not always popular. In polarized issues empathy can become suspect. Gentleness is weak. Courtesy is compromise.

But I have never thought so. Certainly reason does not have to undermine emotion. Roger illustrates this when he tells the story of the Inuit Qisuk and his son Minik who traveled with the Arctic explorer Robert Peary to New York in 1897. Here Qisuk fell ill and died. Doctors promptly dissected his body, removed his brain, and boiled the flesh from his bones.

"But the staff at the American Museum of Natural History had a problem," Roger says. "They had this little Inuit boy who had suddenly lost his father. So they arranged a phony funeral so Minik would believe his father had been respectfully buried. Later Qisuk's bones were put on display."

In 1906 the Antiquities Act defined Indian remains as "archaeological resources." In the 1910s Minik returned to the American Museum of Natural History.

"Can you imagine," Roger asks us, "how you would feel, seeing your father there, like that?"

When Roger is silent, I suspect this is unprogrammed. I believe he is briefly unable to speak, possibly near tears. I know that his own father is dead and that the gift of his father's library, filled with books on Pawnee culture, began Roger's career as a tribal historian. My father, a test pilot in the 1950s, is also dead, and I remember seeing with pride a plaque with his name on it in the Smithsonian Museum of Space and Aviation. How would I have felt, instead, if they had hung up his skeleton?

Outraged, deeply saddened, Minik asked for his father's remains. He was refused. (Qisuk's bones were reburied, finally, in Greenland in 1993.)

A few years after Minik's death, in the 1920s, an am-
ateur archaeologist and used-car salesman named Asa Hill
began promoting the excavation of Pawnee villages and
burial grounds throughout Nebraska and Kansas. Inspired
by dramatic discoveries in Egypt, Asa Hill, "the father of
Nebraska archaeology," became director of the Nebraska
State Historical Society Museum with its growing collection of skeletal remains. At some point the museum
briefly took possession of a silver medal, looted from the
body of the Skidi Pawnee Man Chief.

Flash forward sixty years. Roger Echo-Hawk's
brother is Walter Echo-Hawk, an attorney for the Native
American Rights Fund and a national leader in repatriation efforts. In 1986 Walter came to Roger for advice. A
Kansas tourist attraction featured the skeletons of nearly
200 ancestral Pawnee, hand-shellacked and artfully arranged, advertised on a highway bulletin board as an
"Authentic Prehistoric Indian Burial Pit, Left, Next
Exit." School teachers brought their classes to the Pit.
Motorists stopped to buy milkshakes and a hot dog. A
coalition of Pawnee, Arikara, and Wichita were trying to
close the exhibit and pass a law protecting Indian grave
sites in Kansas. The state historical society, the state archaeologist, and the state attorney all supported the
bill—which failed. Roger is matter-of-fact. "State legis-
lators were reluctant to see a viable business shut down."
In 1989 a second bill was successful, and over 100

Pawnee watched the Kansas governor join them in a reburial ceremony.

"For me," Roger says, "the process started."

By now the Pawnee were also talking with the Nebraska State Historical Society Museum concerning its
remains and burial artifacts. These discussions did not go
well. The director of the museum believed that human
remains before 1750 were "culturally anonymous." He
claimed "a custodial ownership" of the material and
questioned the Pawnee's religious sincerity, suggesting
they might sell the grave goods rather than rebury them.
He insisted that scientists needed access to this collection.
Aggressively, he took the high ground, "I consider the
destruction of scientific information to be morally and
ethically reprehensible, and that is exactly what is being
demanded of us."

In the legal struggle that followed, the historical society denied the Pawnee access to public records and ignored the advice of their own state attorney. They fought
hard every step of the way, and they lost. A reburial bill
not only passed in Nebraska, it received wide public support. In one newspaper poll seven out of ten Nebraskans
agreed with the Pawnee.

Larry Zimmerman, an archaeologist from South
Dakota, helped the tribe establish its relationship to skeletons 1,000 years old. "This case and others made archaeologists wake up," Larry says. "Suddenly they realized that
the general public did not know what archaeology was
doing with all these skeletal remains and did not really
think it was very important. Most people could more eas-

ily understand the Native American point of view. That surprised Indians and archaeologists both."

In 1989 a federal law established the National Museum of the American Indian and prodded the Smithsonian Institution to return its over 18,000 remains to the appropriate tribes. Roger Echo-Hawk and James Riding In, another tribal historian, went to Washington, D.C., to identify Pawnee material. They also stopped by the National Museum of Health and Medicine, formerly the Army Medical Museum. There they discovered two skulls taken from Pawnee scouts who had fought beside the U.S. Army against the Sioux. These men were part of a unit organized with the approval of the Pawnee tribe as a symbol of their alliance with the United States. Military veterans are particularly honored among the Pawnee. Emotionally, Roger and James asked for the skulls' return. That small mission failed.

In September of 1990 the remains of 400 Pawnee were taken in coffins from the Nebraska State Historical Society Museum. A few months later the passage of the Native American Graves Protection and Repatriation Act (NAGPRA) ensured that all institutions receiving federal funding or support would cooperate with repatriation requests. Soon after, the former Army Medical Museum contacted the Pawnee: they could have the two skulls.

"NAGPRA embodied all the goals that Indians had set," Roger says. "It was the result of a lot of battles, small skirmishes and big skirmishes. By and large, what happened in Nebraska and Kansas and what happened in

Congress was a victory, a real victory. It was also, at times, a bitter and troubling experience."

When Roger stops talking, the students applaud. Roger, too, has been a student at the University of Colorado, where he received a master's degree in history. His thesis tries to reconcile archaeology with oral tradition, which he believes can go back more than 10,000 years, to the days of the Pleistocene. Many Native American origin stories begin with "dark worlds" that may refer to the Arctic Circle and the land bridge crossed by the first band of Mongoloids. Other stories seem to describe glacial ice sheets and dramatic weather patterns associated with the end of the Pleistocene. Diverse tribes talk of monsters that could be memories of extinct animals like the mammoth and giant short-faced bear.

"I question the assumption that societies 'forget' every aspect of their past with the passage of enough time," Roger says. "There is no good, valid reason to think so. Verbal literature is extremely durable. A serious look at oral tradition could provide a whole new set of information for scholars."

Roger looks at myths from around the world that might be connected to Pleistocene events. He thinks that North American tales may stretch back all the way to Asia. In some cases the marriage of science and oral tradition can have very specific results; a Cowichan memory of ice sheets at Puget Sound could place settlement of that area at 15,000 to 28,000 B.P.

"This kind of analysis," Roger says, "has tremendous potential."

By now many archaeologists would be jumping from their chairs, checking their watches, or thinking about lunch. Archaeology's neglect of oral history borders on disdain.

"An important result of academic inquiry into the distant past," Roger says, "has been to people the world of that past with voiceless human figures. In that view people never talked to each other about what they were doing. But people *were* talking to each other. There has been an unbroken chain of conversation up to the present."

Like others who walk in the middle of the road, Roger finds that the traffic comes from both directions. Archaeologists deny tradition. Traditional Indians deny archaeological evidence that undermines tribal beliefs. In particular, the idea that Native Americans crossed the Bering Strait from Asia counters specific origin tales—that the Oglala sprang from the caves of the Black Hills or the Tohono O'odham from Mount Baboquivari or the Nez Perce from Kakayohneme Creek.

"There's no doubt in my mind that archaeologists have a role to play in understanding our ancient history," Roger says. "But there are still many Indians, many Indian intellectuals and religious leaders, who are very much opposed to archaeology as a profession. I run into that all the time, although attitudes are swiftly changing. Still, there's a vocal element in most Indian communities that says these guys are oppressors, they are not sensitive, they are part of the problem. I understand the source of this sentiment. But I think we need to move forward, into a partnership with archaeologists.

"I see areas of common interest. I see a lot of hope that changes will not be limited to specific issues of repatriation but will lead to the larger question. What is the nature of archaeology's relationship with Indians and what should it be?"

At the end of his thesis, Roger writes, "For those who desire to find common ground in a complex world, my wish is that they will discover here an unsuspected passage to a whole new world, a new world in which we are united rather than forever divided on our various continents, a world in which we share the quest to understand our origins as humans, as Native Americans, and as the citizens of a truly multicultural, global village. This, I believe, is a good wish."

ABOVE THE MISSOURI RIVER in South Dakota, things were getting desperate for a group of ancestral Arikara: too many people, not enough buffalo, not enough corn. Children born here at Crow Creek in the fourteenth century likely suffered from seasonal malnutrition and diseases like scurvy. Scarce resources promoted war, and the village was well fortified against attack. But when the raiders came, there must have been many of them, heavily armed. Easily they broached the hand-dug ditch and wooden stockade, killing, scalping, and mutilating over 500 men, women, and children inside. Later the survivors crept back to bury their dead in a hasty, mass grave.

In 1978 the remains of these victims were being disturbed by natural erosion and local pothunters. Archaeol-

ogists, the Corp of Engineers, and the Crow Creek Sioux
Tribal Council agreed to stabilize the area. Scientists
would be allowed twelve months to excavate and study
the bones before reburial. Soon the story of the ancient
massacre became a media event. Thousands of Native
Americans and Anglos visited the site. On the nearby
Sioux reservation, feelings were mixed. At one point archaeologists had to be pulled from the field when their
lives were threatened. Then a Sioux holy man built a
sweat lodge near the excavation and released any *wanagi'*,
or malevolent spirits, guarding the graves. Some Sioux
still did not want the remains to leave the reservation for
analysis. Others did not want Arikara buried on Sioux
land. At the same time the site's physical anthropologist
felt the time allowed for study was too short. Outside archaeologists also criticized the project for its "unrealistic
deadlines" and overenthusiastic support of reburial.

For Larry Zimmerman, one of the chief archaeologists, this was an initiatory experience.

"In dealing with the Indians I saw a whole range of
views," Larry remembers. "Some supported our excavation. Others said that my crew would be killed if we continued. I learned quickly the intensity of Indian feelings
for the ancestors. With young, yelling militants you can
easily suspect political motivations, but when you hear
the pleas of elders and holy people, you know that other,
deeply felt spiritual concerns are at work.

"Many Native Americans, through some sort of
Pan-Indian redefinition of sacredness, now consider all
human skeletal material to be sacred. It doesn't matter if

these remains are only distantly related or not related at all. Archaeologists complain that this is a recent invention. So? We are dealing with a contemporary religion. Pan-Indian or not, it's their belief now. As anthropologists, we should respect the fact that cultures change. We shouldn't try to lock Indians into the past."

In 1982 Jan Hammil-BearShield, director of American Indians Against Desecration, asked Larry Zimmerman to accompany her and the American Indian Movement to the yearly Society for American Archaeology conference. There he was to present "the positive aspects of working with Indians." After a number of meetings the group persuaded the SAA to postpone passing an antireburial resolution. (They passed it the next year and rescinded it six months later.) Meanwhile, Larry's true colors were revealed. He was an Indian wanna-be, a radical, and a troublemaker. On his part, Larry seriously considered quitting archaeology.

"Our first concern is protecting our own turf," he wrote in 1989. "Our concern for those we study is minimal, and persists as long as it does not interfere with what we do . . . we are sometimes very racist as a profession. We do not like to hear ourselves called that, and I am certain that racism is not our intent. But from the perspective of the Indians we most certainly are. We use every tactic in the book to protect the great archaeological myth we call 'data.' "

These tactics begin with the insistence that only archaeology and its scientific method can interpret the past—a denial of oral history, song, and ritual. Archaeol-

ogists minimize cultural affiliation by emphasizing the
time that separates modern and ancient Indians. They
exploit the diversity of Native American cultures and re-
fuse to recognize universal themes. Hypocritically they
complain about "lost data" when they know that excavation itself is destructive; the loss of some data has always
been acceptable.

Larry believes that archaeologists and Native Americans have two different views on two important subjects.

"Archaeologists view the past as something com-
prised of linear starts and stops, something which must be
excavated and studied to be understood. For many Indians the past simply is. It is continuous, and forms the
present, and perhaps guides the future. It need not be
studied because it is always with you. The law is similar.
Archaeologists tend to view the law in terms of a method
for the settlement of disputes. We use it to talk about
abandoned cemeteries, precedents, and the like. Many
Indians, though they can use the white legal system effec-
tively, view the law as something given by god or the spirits that is timeless and immutable. When we get into
meetings with Indians, both sides can be using the same
terms and simply talk right past each other. We are the
ones supposed to be trained in cross-cultural matters, but
we apparently have difficulty seeing the problem.

"Sometimes the sense of frustration is high and ends
with one side yelling at the other. Most archaeologists
seem to fear the yelling, perhaps because they believe it
demonstrates their failure as anthropologists. I think being yelled at by my colleagues and Indians is good for the

soul. The archaeological penchant for 'civility' tends to force what is in every way an emotional issue into an analytical framework. Anger, especially when one is the recipient, can open one's thinking."

"Now," Larry says, "I find being yelled at exhilarating. I know what it can lead to. Anger releases the tension. Then, if you have people on both sides courageous enough to say, 'Well, that's over,' you can get down to brass tacks."

Over the years, these are some of the voices that have yelled at Larry Zimmerman.

Sioux Maria D. Pearson: "We Indians respect our ancestors. They are present in our ceremonies and we call upon them for help to live our lives helping one another. Perhaps the archaeologist and the physical anthropologist don't feel that way. However, who made them supreme? Who gave them the right to ignore our beliefs and wishes? If digging graves is so important, why not dig up white graves? The difference is simply this. To this kind of person, the Indian isn't really human, their dead have no rights, and their living descendants should be honored to have some grave robber dig up their ancestors and, if they ever get around to doing anything with the remains, write lengthy and terribly complex papers in terms understandable only to a professional archaeologist which are filed in libraries and read only by other archaeologists when forced to do so as part of some other grave robbery."

Mescalero Apache Jan Hammil-BearShield: "We believe in an afterlife. That which is called death, to us, is only a change in life as we continue on a journey to the spirit world and thereby become one with our Mother, the Earth. Any disruption, delay, or halt in that journey is a violation of personal religious beliefs to that individual, to his descendants who incorporate and are responsible for his spirit in their daily lives and religious ceremonies, and to those of the present and the future who will embark on that journey."

Potawatomi Ben Rhodd: "Our world view cannot allow for disturbance. Disturbance unbalances the universe. This is pretty basic and simple. It has to do with the will of the people and the interests of the land, not an intellectual argument. It deals with a spiritual way of life."

Pima Cecil Antone: "Archaeologists don't know the way of life of the Native Americans that live on the reservation, to know what is there for them, what is provided by the Creator. You will never know that. You will never know in your life what the land means to the Indian people. You've just got one thing in mind, and that's the almighty dollar. This land was made for my ancestors, not your ancestors. That is why this land is respected. But since the infiltration of white society into this country, it is slowly dribbling down. And those people who lived here many years ago were brought here by the Creator. We are trying to take care of those people that were here. They are a part of us."

Many archaeologists have also wanted to yell at Larry Zimmerman.

Lynne Goldstein says, "The anthropological or scientific worldview can be seen as a cultural construction in which the excavation and curation of human skeletal remains is both proper and necessary. To put it simply, anthropology has a system of ethics beyond the notion that we have certain obligations to those we study. Eliminating sites or portions of sites from excavation or analysis because of the kind of items they contain is not an ethical stance for an archaeologist. . . . We have a mandate to preserve and protect the past for the future—an obligation to past cultures to tell their story and to future generations to preserve the past for their benefit. It is part of the culture of archaeology that we, as archaeologists, view ourselves as the stewards of the past."

Clement Meighan writes, "As for the roots of the movement, there is a considerable anti-intellectual strain present. It is asserted that museums have done nothing for Indians, that researchers do not report their findings to Indians, that universities are squirreling things away for their own gratification, that people who study skeletons must be necrophiles, that whites do not study their own bones and artifacts, etc. All of these statements are demonstrably false, but this refrain is popular with some politicians who can bash intellectuals and appear at the same time to be supporting minority interests (by symbolic actions which don't cost them anything)."

Clement Meighan believes that too many reburials are politically inspired and politically resolved. He is angry when "a 1/128 Indian from the eastern United States" tries to lay claim to burial remains and artifacts in California. He compares the larger controversy to the teaching of evolution in the public schools: when should religion dictate science and education?

In 1993, when a state archaeologist returned for reburial a 10,000-year-old skeleton to the Shoshone-
Bannock tribe, Clement Meighan found himself yelling,
"They're throwing away one of the two or three major
finds in the New World. . . . We're talking about a skeleton that was around 5,000 years before the pyramids of
Egypt were built. Repatriation is a loaded and improper
term because it implies that you're giving something back
to people who own it. They don't own it and never did."

Even archaeologists sympathetic to Native Americans can feel frustrated. At the Newark Earthworks in
Ohio, Brad Lepper once tried to dig a test trench
through the Great Circle to determine its age. This was
not a burial site, and no tribal group complained. But
Indians living in nearby Columbus—a Tewa, a Yaqui, a
Sioux—brought in TV cameras for a series of dubious
ceremonies. The yelling became virulent. Of course,
Brad Lepper had begun his excavation in a year powerfully and symbolically charged: 1992, the Columbian
Quincentenary.

"We often say that it's only political," Larry Zimmerman says. "Well, of course it is! Politics and the sacred
often coalesce. Sure, some of this has been about power.
It's about control. Archaeologists, certainly, have been
afraid to lose the control they've previously enjoyed."

It's time to get down to brass tacks.

"In another ten years," Larry Zimmerman predicts,
"this will be water over the dam. In the last five years I've
seen things change so incredibly fast. You know, the professional perception of me is that I'm too negative. But

I'm actually the opposite. I'm an optimist. A cynical optimist? I know that we archaeologists have a right to our human foibles. We have a right to be protective of what we hold dear. It's just too bad this had to happen the hard way, that we had to be dragged kicking and screaming to Congress to get a law shoved down our throats. But now I think we are making progress. A lot of people have made a reasonable transition or are in the process of making one.

"This is all about change. Working with Roger and Jan and Maria has made me understand things that are outside my normal scope of cultural perception. It's challenged my view of the world. And that's good. Yes, change means that we will lose some things. We will lose access to some remains, some bones, some collections. We will lose some opportunities for analysis. But we don't have to lose everything. It's not all or nothing. We have to work with Native Americans, case by case. In the end, what we gain—what we gain—is so much greater than what we lose."

NEW LAWS HAVE TRANSFORMED the practice of archaeology. But we can't legislate good will.

"I don't trust legislation," Iroquois archaeologist Louis Redmond says. "I don't think it's the answer. I'm one of those people who drives ten miles above the speed limit. I push the legislative envelope. That's what will happen to NAGPRA. Only a dialogue between Native Americans and archaeologists is going to work, especially between archaeologists and tribal elders."

Louis Redmond makes sense to me, perhaps because I also drive above the speed limit, sixty-five when the sign says fifty-five, seventy-five on the flat black interstates that shrink distance in the American West. Today, however, on the Navajo reservation, I prefer to go slowly, staring out my car window.

I do not want to leave this landscape behind. I want to stay right here, locked in embrace with these sweeps of yellow-green grass against red soil hills. At the horizon, chalky cliffs form shapes like a cloud bank. I know these Southwestern colors very well. I learned them in childhood, as familiar as a camp song, and I live beside them now in the Mimbres Valley, where the eroded pink cliffs twist into canyons. The crinkled land is dotted with juniper, scrub oak, and chamisa. Green and pink, red and green. Looking closer, I can see in the rock shades of lavender, orange, yellow, rainbows of rock in a country where rock dominates, slick rock, cliff rock, rock flowing up like sheets of water.

But rock is not water, and this land is dry, hot, spare. A small group of people might live here from the rabbits and antelope, from a herd of sheep, a goat, and a patch of corn. But this land cannot be tamed like the Midwest. This is not the lush East or the abundant coast. This is land you love, unrequited, for its solitary strength and extravagant beauty.

At Window Rock, the capital of the Navajo Nation, I follow Larry Benallie's instructions to the Navajo Nation Tribal Park. The town's landmark is a massive stone arch over 100 feet tall, a window into blue sky and a background for Navajo teens just out of school, listening to rap music. I pass the impressive Tribal President's office, some gorgeous red stone buildings, and a line of bright yellow Head Start buses. Behind the motor pool is a two-story wooden shoebox with a sign: The Navajo Nation Archaeology Department. It's an unprepossessing place for a department that handles 3 million dollars of work a year, employing over fifty people with the responsibility for over 16 million acres that contain an estimated 1.5 million archaeological sites. Inside, the office is cheerfully grungy. A set of window blinds look like they've been attacked by a bored Siamese. Larry Benallie, assistant director, sits in front of his computer. Behind him the radio plays a version of "Help"—not a bad remake, but not the Beatles.

Part-Navajo, part-Hopi, Larry Benallie was a junior at Window Rock High School when he got a summer job at a highway excavation near Pinon. Traditional Navajos believe that touching human bones and burial goods can make a living person physically and spiritually sick. Right away the archaeologist on the site asked the teenager, "Are you afraid of dead things?"

Today Larry asks me, "Do you know rock and roll? Well, this guy looked like the character on the Jethro Tull *Aqualung* album." This isn't an insult. Larry says fondly that he "learned a lot. I loved the work. It was fun, fascinating. I went on to get my B.A. in anthropology at Penn State and M.A. in archaeology at Arizona State University. It's different for Native Americans because you are studying your own people, your own culture. It makes you more self-aware. This past history, it's history that is still living. It's what makes you who you are."

Among Navajos Larry's view is probably the exception. On the reservation archaeology remains "a necessary evil." Here the construction of any water line, power line, or road is a federal project that falls under the National Historic Preservation Act of 1966. First there must be an archaeological survey, then the avoidance or excavation of any significant site. At the same time, in remote areas like Chinle and Pinon, basic services are very much needed. Some 70 percent of the reservation still has no electricity.

"We have to do archaeology for development," Larry says. "But we don't want it to be a hindrance. We try to do our work as fast, as thoroughly as possible. Sometimes we get berated as a profession. Indian people get mad at us, and they have a legitimate gripe. Archaeologists have been really arrogant in the past. Still, Indians want these sites protected. They don't want them desecrated. I think it's only natural that Indians should be doing this work on Indian land, that *I* should be doing it."

Navajo archaeology is different. When construction disturbs a grave site, reburial is automatic. "On the spot," Larry says, "with no destructive analysis. Some of the department's staff won't go near that kind of work. And professionally, that's okay. I've had to do reburials myself. All the time I'm thinking, 'I'm sorry, I'm sorry, I'm sorry, this is something that has to be done.' As a Navajo archaeologist, I've had to make certain inner deals. I've had to work this out in my mind. Combining scientific evidence with tradition can be hard. Of course," Larry pauses. He has a sweet grin; now it's a bit wry. "I don't think archaeology is exactly a *science*."

Science, here, is not the magic touchstone. Archaeology is "a history still living," something that requires constant consultation with modern tribes. Medicine men naturally visit the department to evaluate artifacts or open medicine bundles. That seems obvious. But Larry remembers his last archaeology conference when a woman pondered at length the meaning of certain "protohistoric Navajo structures." Larry wonders why she hadn't talked to local Navajos. "They could have told her a lot," he says, "if she had asked. But archaeologists don't usually ask. They're afraid to ask. They're afraid to offend people or to get into some kind of trouble. Just as often, they don't want to spend the time."

In the 1980s when Larry Benallie was getting his degrees, he was "the only Indian in the classroom." Now his department has a student training program that encourages Navajos to take anthropology and archaeology classes and to graduate in those fields.

Davina TwoBears is such a student. She introduces herself as the product of lineage, "My maternal clan is *Todich'ii'nii*, Bitter Water clan, and I am born for *Tachii'nii*, Red Running into the Water clan. My maternal grandfather is also *Todich'ii'nii*. My mother's family is from the community of Bird Springs, Arizona, on the Navajo reservation. My parents are Tom and Anita Ryan."

With an M.A. in anthropology Davina struggles to keep her balance. "Our profession is often considered impractical, disrespectful, and misleading or incorrect by most Native Americans," she writes for an article in the SAA newsletter. "I'll be honest in admitting that I feel the same. . . . It is hard, as a Native American, to be the object of study. At anthropology conferences, I often feel like a walking specimen to be photographed, documented, measured, and dissected. It's a strange feeling to think that so many non-Native American scientists find us Indians interesting objects of study, and that they would go so far as to write books about us, and then as "experts" talk about us to other scientists at conferences. It makes one feel as though a Native American is not even a person or human but just a very complex, interesting thing."

Davina TwoBears sees her work from two shifting perspectives, outside the glass, looking in, and inside the glass, looking out. She changes focus so rapidly her vision blurs.

"I think our profession will only improve with increased participation of the people whom we study," she says, "and by giving something back to them."

In this case, them is us, she is them.

Like other Native American professionals, Davina may be more interested in service than science. "When I'm driving on the res, it's nice to see the places where I conducted archaeological surveys, now developed with homes, electricity, and water. I know that I helped make it happen for my people."

She believes that "Native Americans who become anthropologists and archaeologists can only benefit our tribes and Native Americans in general. We can determine what is appropriate to publish and what is not. We can determine how and what is to be exhibited in museums. We can determine what gets studied, photographed, recorded, and what should be left alone. We can determine what should get excavated, if at all, and how it should be done."

These kinds of statements scare some people. Almost everyone agrees that more Native Americans should become archaeologists. (Larry Zimmerman was delighted to pass on his trowel to a Winnebago student, so that she could excavate Crusader burials in Israel.) But almost everyone does not want the logical result. Archaeologists expect to educate Indians; they do not expect to be educated in turn.

Yet this is what happens, what must happen, whenever collaborations are successful.

In Washington, tribes have long worked with people like Dale Croes, who regularly has his sites blessed and who can say with ease, "They know more about the spirit than we do." On the Atlantic Coast, when the Massachusetts Archaeological Society invited Native Americans to their board, they met around a campfire on the Wampanoag reservation and used the "Talking Stick" method for discussion. A field school in Connecticut is jointly offered by a local university and the Mohegan. The Pima and Makah are happy to learn curation skills as they create cultural centers that redefine the nature of a museum. Similarly, many tribes like the Sioux use archaeology to substantiate land claims. A Hopi prophecy foresees a time when even the ashes of the ancestors will help the tribe; some Hopi link this to the floatation analysis of ancient hearths.

Across the country the dialogue between tribal elders, nontraditional Indians, and archaeologists has begun. Like Larry Zimmerman and Larry Benallie, the people who work on these projects find their view of the world challenged. They hear the echo of their own question: who are you?

I stand near an ancient site, a small hill on the Zuni reservation, sixty miles from Window Rock. Easily I can follow the lines of stone where houses once stood. Amid low-growing prickly pear and wolfberry, I see discernable fire hearths. Below, the land gently slopes into a valley luminous with the new growth of spring. Pink and green, green and red. Massive bluffs rise up like ships cresting this emerald ocean. The flat-topped mesas are surreal. Extravagant beauty. It can break your heart.

Standing next to me, Roger Anyon has been an archaeologist at Zuni for ten years. The Zunis also excavate only when forced to by construction and development. Roger is a tall thin Englishman with a single earring, a simple design of silver and turquoise. He talks about the potsherds that cover the ground.

"The Zunis gather these and grind them up and use them as temper for new pots. That's part of the cycle for them. When they find an arrowhead on the reservation, they pick it up and use it as a necklace, to ward off witches, many uses. This drives some archaeologists crazy. 'They're destroying the archaeological record,' " he mimics a horrified colleague. "They just don't get it."

Roger has changed in the last ten years. Like Davina TwoBears, he struggles now to keep his balance. "I used to be a heavy-duty science type, a real processualist. The Zunis cured me of that problem. Scientists think they are objective. But the cultural loading in archaeology is unbelievable. Many people who do science don't understand the limits of science. They have this amazing tunnel vision. Archaeologists should sit down and admit, 'I like what I'm doing and it's fun and it's how I think about the world. But it's not objective and it's not necessarily how the world works.'

"Archaeology is an intellectual pursuit. It satisfies an intellectual curiosity. But for Zunis, life is experiential, not intellectual. The dances and the ceremonies here go on all the time. They are all about experience. We Anglos are still living out the Enlightenment. We live with that cultural baggage, that split between the mind and body. Zunis don't split things up like that."

Unlike Roger Echo-Hawk, Roger Anyon does not see much common ground between archaeologists and Indians—at least, not between archaeologists and traditional Zunis. Yes, they both want to stop the desecration and looting of sites, but for very different reasons.

"The Zunis believe in four stages of life. In this life, we are only in the first stage. The people buried in these sites are still on a journey. The journey is over when all the bones and all the grave goods are completely dissolved into the earth. So, wherever burials are, people are on journeys. It's going on now. It's in the present, not in the past. Those sites are not inanimate. They are not alive ex-

actly, but they are imbued with life forces. Whatever information we get from these sites has to be weighed
against what it will do to the people buried there and
what it will do to you as a person who destroys or inter-
rupts this cycle.

"Archaeologists want to save sites for future excavation and research. But unless it is absolutely necessary,
most Zunis don't want any excavation of any site. It's important to recognize this, to see how different we are."

The wind picks up. The red rocks rise grandly, un-
speakably beautiful, against blue and green. We stay on
the hill, staring out, unwilling to leave.

"This place where we are standing," Roger says, "is
doing what it is supposed to do just by being here. It's not
supposed to be disturbed."

Roger is an archaeologist who no longer wants to
dig up sites. "Construction produces more than enough
archaeology. Academics need to dig a lot less and be
smarter about their research. We ask a lot of inappropriate
questions and that produces a lot of meaningless, mind-
numbing information. We need to completely restruc-
ture, reinvent archaeology."

A deep arroyo now cuts the middle of this valley. A
Zuni family is going to their cornfield. We watch their
truck carefully dip down, disappear, and come up the
other side.

"Archaeologists need to use what they learn to reflect
on their own culture, their own time," Roger says. "What
is the point if we don't learn something about ourselves?"

I reshape that question. It's another good wish.

IN OUR GRANDMOTHER'S HOUSE

IN MOST RELIGIOUS TRADITIONS THE WORLD IS whole, and humans are not in charge. For many of us today the world has been broken into confusing parts for which we are directly responsible. We must save the rainforest, clean up the rivers, prevent soil erosion, close the hole in the sky, limit our population growth—and watch for hot viruses. Undereducated and undertrained, we are the middle managers of a very complicated planet. We feel plagued by doubt and office burnout. Our sense of urgency increases. Maybe we were promoted too fast? Maybe we're not management material?

American archaeologists have a similar headache. Roads, houses, factories, farms, restaurants, shopping malls, office buildings, parking lots, tennis courts, and swimming pools are stripping away our archaeological record. An exploding interest in "primitive and prehistoric art" means that many sites are also being looted. By necessity archaeology has become dominated by the phrase CRM, or Cultural Resource Management, a changing system of laws that regulate how we deal with ancient artifacts and remains. The linchpin remains the National Historic Preservation Act of 1966, which mandated federal agencies to seek out and conserve important archaeological sites. In 1979 the Archaeological Resources Protection Act further defined cultural resources on public land and set penalties for vandalism and looting. NAGPRA helped clarify the legal relationship of some artifacts and remains to modern tribes. Other rules and regulations try to fill in the holes and alleviate our basic bewilderment—how do we "manage the past?"

Perhaps more than any academic field, archaeology has been absorbed into a government bureaucracy. Archaeologists like Joanne Dickenson, Todd Bostwick, Brad Lepper, Larry Benallie, and Roger Anyon work for a variety of tribal, federal, state, or city agencies. Their jobs range from educating the public to tracking down pothunters. Paperwork is no longer a research project. The telephone has invaded the ivory tower.

Because of CRM, archaeology is also a business. When federal laws require a survey of potential sites, it is often contracted out to a private company. If a site must be excavated, that is also often done through bids and contracts. State laws may require a "licensed archaeologist" to deal with human remains on private land. The yellow pages of any phone book in any major city have a new listing: archaeological services.

But CRM is not just a new part of archaeology; it is the largest part. Perhaps one out of a hundred students graduating with a degree in archaeology will find a job as a university professor, an academic like Pat Watson or Kathleen Deagan involved in teaching or pure research. The other ninety-nine will go into some form of CRM.

Catherine Cameron (whose husband is Steve Lekson) is on the President's Advisory Council on Historic Preservation, established to help federal agencies conform to national laws. "We have the best program for historic preservation in the world," Cathy says—as a prelude to saying something quite different.

Our preservation program worked, for example, when the Central Arizona Project spent 4 billion dollars to bring Colorado River water to farms, cities, and Indian communities in central Arizona. The construction included a 330-mile-long canal and a huge distribution network, as well as new dams and reservoirs. By 1995, 35 million dollars had been diverted into archaeology.

Lynn Teague was head of the CRM Division at the Arizona State Museum at the University of Arizona. She directed the work on a major aqueduct in a river valley filled with Hohokam sites. "It was very stressful," she remembers. "At one point we had more than a hundred people on the project, in the field. We had deadlines, deadlines, like you always do in CRM. I was out working all the time. Finally I had to go to the doctor. When the nurse called back, she said the results were positive. 'Which ones?' I asked. 'Oh, all of them,' she said, 'You have strep throat, Valley Fever, pneumonia . . .' " Lynn laughs.

"But we learned a tremendous amount. No one had ever dug these kinds of sites before, these small outlying settlements. In the 1960s you could have held a meeting of Hohokam archaeologists in your bathroom. Now we have big conferences. We've totally revised our understanding of Hohokam history and chronology. It's going on right now. All this contract and CRM work is producing a tremendous amount of information.

"When I started, CRM was just taking off, driven by laws that were so new no one had a handle on them. The University of Arizona was doing the contract work then, with maybe a half-dozen people. By the early 1980s we were employing as many as 180. We eventually stopped because private companies grew to the point where we couldn't compete—and we didn't have to. The companies around here are excellent."

Lynn Teague jokes that she was "one of those good little girls" who went into archaeology because it allowed her to get dirty. After fifteen years the thrill wore off. Today she is out of the field and in charge of repatriation for the state of Arizona. She echoes Todd Bostwick: things are going smoothly. "Developers often find it really interesting when tribal elders come to do a ceremony or a prayer on their construction site. They are getting to meet new types of people." She repeats Larry Zimmerman. "Archaeologists benefit more from getting closer to these cultures in their living form than whatever they lost in any kind of analysis." She agrees with Larry Benallie. "The native peoples of Arizona have a right to manage their own heritage. There are some things a tribe might wish that aren't my personal preference. But that's not the issue. I don't doubt their right to make these decisions."

Like Lynn, most CRM archaeologists have no territory to protect, no research questions they must control. Reburial is simple. It's the law. CRM often aligns with the Native American view because it is essentially preservationist. Sites are dug when they are imperiled, because they are imperiled.

Although cultural resource management usually takes place outside the university, it can still further research. Salvage archaeology produces information that would otherwise be lost. Sometimes government agencies and private companies have more money to use state-of-the-art technology. Also, they are geared toward publication. They must produce a timely written report. CRM archaeologists don't procrastinate or hoard data. They are on a deadline. They go on to the next project.

Cathy Cameron drops the other shoe. For a successful program, "the best in the world," CRM has a lot of critics.

"Oh, in Arizona," Cathy says, "they've done some wonderful work. Fantastic stuff. But in other states the situation can be horrible. We have this continuum from wonderful to horrible. We have to bring everyone up to the same level."

Cathy thinks CRM is "a program that's broken." She rattles off the ways. "Students at the university aren't being trained in CRM. They graduate without the slightest idea how to do this kind of work. All these reports, the gray literature that CRM produces, isn't widely available. Academic archaeologists aren't using the material appropriately. When we're talking contract archaeology, by private businesses, there's no interactive monitoring. No one is peer-reviewing the data. Most of all, CRM isn't tied to anything larger, to any larger picture. There's no effort or money to synthesize the information. It can get very costly, all this feature-by-feature excavation. A road goes in here, and so we excavate these sites. But it's work that's not always done well or that gives us particularly good information. We have to be more accountable. These preservation laws have to benefit the public or they could go away. They could be repealed. *That* would be a disaster."

Most of these problems have solutions. They require creativity—and cooperation. Archaeology has any number of schisms; the one between CRM and academia may be the most self-destructive. One side is accused of being unprofessional and commercial. The other is labeled elitist and impractical. They have, at times, very different interests. A tribal archaeologist believes that a non-threatened site should never be excavated. A private contract company tries to maximize its profits by doing as much archaeology as possible. A professor wants particular research done as a way of furthering his or her career.

As the bulldozer approaches, CRM archaeologists, academics, and Native Americans can hardly afford to be in the middle of an argument.

"Archaeology is an expensive activity that requires public support," Catherine Cameron says. "Americans have a right to good archaeology for their money, with some sort of cost-benefit analysis."

Recently, funding for the Advisory Council and for the entire National Historic Preservation Act was threatened by budget cuts in Congress. In the "management of the past," both nouns are cultural constructions, open to interpretation. "We don't manage the past," Roger Anyon says, "we manage the present."

Who expected it to be easy?

ALLEN FUNKHOUSER wears his gun even in the halls of the Gila National Forest Supervisor's Office, decorated with happy pictures of Smoky the Bear. Allen is a criminal investigator for the Forest Service in southern New Mexico. Crime in the Gila includes drug traffic, theft, range trespass, and the looting of archeological resources. For thousands of years Mogollon and Mimbres tribes lived in this area, and their sites still scatter these 3 million acres of public land. The people who work in this office have a reputation for vigorously pursuing pothunters. James Adovasio, from the Meadowcroft Rock Shelter, calls them "rabid." That's a compliment.

No one knows how much of our archaeological heritage is being stolen, because no one knows how much we have left. A 1987 government report estimated that only 7 percent of sites had been surveyed on America's 104 million acres of Forest Service, Bureau of Land Management, and National Park Service land. In 1989 a group of federal land managers concluded that vandals and thieves had damaged at least 90 percent of known sites in the Southwest, including almost all of the Classic Mimbres sites. Another estimate is that 50 percent of sites on American public and private land have been destroyed.

For the archaeologist the loss is profound. "Analyzing a site," Catherine Cameron says, "is like the reconstruction of a crime scene. The context in which artifacts and structures are found is vitally important to understanding the culture of which they were once a part. Artifacts out of context may appear beautiful, exotic, or mundane, but they have lost their power to tell the story of past peoples and cultures."

Much of the damage is done by professional looters. Allen Funkhouser describes a scene both similar and tied to drug dealing. Often the same people are involved, an organized network of criminals whose buyers are commonly overseas. Working at night on isolated public land, pothunters can make a tremendous amount of money. Locally, an especially fine Classic Mimbres bowl might fetch $1,000; sold in Albuquerque, it could net $45,000; auctioned in New York, it gets $95,000; taken to Europe, it reaps $400,000.

People like Allen fight back with undercover cops, informants, bullet-proof vests, and back-country Broncos bristling with antennas. They set up sting operations and find themselves leaping into dingy hotel rooms, flashing badges, barking clichés, "Federal officers! Up against the wall!" One National Park Service archaeologist posed as the mistress of a wealthy collector; her fashionable sweater, tank top, and Lycra tights concealed a harness with two mikes and a tape recorder. Deliberately "bitchy," she convinced a pothunter to take her on a helicopter to a looted site. Later she was heard to murmur as she packed away a tiny woven cotton sandal from Utah, stored in an evidence vault in Santa Fe, "Archaeologists *never* find these. *We* find little bits of cloth. Now I know why. Someone has already been there."

Commercial looters are also homegrown. In my valley families have pot hunted Mimbres sites for generations. On private land that's legal. On public land it's not. For some Westerners the difference between private and public land is still confusing. The idea that a dirty pot equals money is still miraculous—a sweet deal for a short day's work.

"At some point they have to sell it or show it," Allen says. "That's where we get them. We go to the dealers, we go to the museums, we go to the sales. If you're going to dig, the chances are good you're going to be caught."

The penalties for getting caught vary. Under the Archaeological Resource Protection Act of 1979, any vehicle or tool used in looting can be seized, with fines up to $100,000 and a year in jail for a misdemeanor, which is defined as damages to a site of $500 or less. For a first felony conviction the fine can be as high as

$250,000, with two years in jail. In reality convictions are few, and judges are lenient. Typically, in 1993, a building supply dealer who looted a rock shelter in the Gila National Forest was fined $5,000, given three years of probation, and ordered to perform 300 hours of community service. Slowly, stiffer sentences are becoming more common.

"But not in the Southwest," Allen admits. "Not yet. We have a culture here that pretty much condones pothunting."

A disincentive that Allen willingly exploits is "hex mythology," the belief in angry spirits who guard Native American graves. "When you are dealing with illegal dealers, they talk about it. There are certain things hard-core diggers won't touch. They might be out there in the forest, and they'll get an eerie feeling. There have been plenty of cases where pothunters have had problems, at the site, or afterwards. When I'm with these guys, I'll say, kind of meaningfully, you take *care* now. Don't get *unlucky*."

At Chaco Canyon the National Park Service warns tourists of misfortunes that befall people who take potsherds. Recently two looters voluntarily confessed to stealing ancient Hopi ceremonial figures—fifteen years ago. They have believed themselves cursed ever since. One man tried burning the kachinas in an effort to lift the spell. Archaeologists who work closely with Native Americans don't scoff. Both Larry Zimmerman and Roger Anyon have had experiences outside their "scope of cultural perception."

Louis Redmond suggests, "When you are on a site, I ask you to act as if you were in your grandmother's house. That's how we view the people who lived there. Be gentle. From some of the things I've seen on desecrated sites, I'd strongly advise it."

Thieves steal because they have customers. Behind the pothunter is the dealer, and behind the dealer is the collector. In the public's eye the first is sinister, the second is sleazy, and the third is cultivated. Amassing large piles of old objects is still something educated upper-class people do to gain status and prestige. Moreover, most of our great public collections have been looted from sites around the world. Often we see these artifacts exhibited as art—beautiful, exotic, out of context.

"The problem with looting is not here in the Four Corners area," one archaeologist told a congressional subcommittee. "It is in the drawing rooms of Washington, D.C., on the mantles of Boston fireplaces, and on the walls of Los Angeles condominiums. . . . Until the reaction to the private display of such artifacts is one of scorn rather than approval, those artifacts will continue to find a market."

Another archaeologist complains of the hypocrisy. "We are saying that it is okay, in fact admirable, for rich people to collect pothunted artifacts and donate them to museums, but it is not okay for destitute Costa Ricans or St. Lawrence islanders to pothunt them or for middle-class artifact dealers in Ohio to trade in them."

If wealthy people are drawn to the cachet of antiquity, so are the poor, the working class, the Boy Scout troop, the senior citizen, the hiker, the biker, the grade school teacher. An important category in pothunting is the casual or hobby collector. One-to-one, commercial looters do more harm. But hobby collectors have a cumulative effect. Huge numbers of people visit our national forests and parks. When a woman on a picnic takes an arrowhead, her act is magnified by a million picnickers. Their interest is often personal, intelligent, and sincere. In that case it can be redirected.

"The real answer is not enforcement," Allen Funkhouser says. "It's public education. We have to get the public on our side or nothing is going to work."

Cautiously Allen sees an improvement. "I think casual pothunting is on the decline or, at least, it has stabilized. We have lots more public archaeology now, site steward programs, Passports in Time, things like that. We go to schools and talk to kids, and I know we're reaching them. We have people come in and confess, 'Hey, I found this basket in a cave, and it was so *neat*, and I took it, but I want to give it back now' or "My family has had these pots for years and I think some of them came from federal land.' We don't prosecute, of course. We're just happy to have the artifacts returned."

As we chat comfortably I don't admit this to Allen Funkhouser, but I am one of the people he has helped educate. There was a time I didn't know that taking a potsherd from the national forest was wrong or illegal. So I did. It was so neat. I had found the Easter egg, the treasure, the thing that sent me spinning back a thousand years. Greedily I desired that little bit of clay. Casually I put it in my pocket. Now I tell my children they may not do this, and I watch their struggle. Like ravens, we are naturally acquisitive. We want to take the magic home.

Instead, my husband and I insist on the archaeological etiquette and say, righteously, "Yes, it's wonderful. It's pretty. Now you've touched it. Now put it back, right where you found it." My children are too young to argue the point. But I understand their resentment. This is, after all, just a broken sherd, a jagged memento, an inch big. This site isn't important, and it isn't pristine. Moreover, the next person who finds this sherd will take it, or the next, or the next. Why not me?

We can hardly imagine a bit of the world not being owned, and so we insist on owning everything, snapping our beaks at the flash of silver. It is a hard lesson—to let things be. It is important, I think, to tell my children, "Put it back where you found it. Leave it alone. Carry it in your mind." It is important to have faith, a belief in each other and in the future, that the next person, and the next, and the millionth will have the same respect and control.

Truthfully, I am not sure that I don't want this bit of earth to dissolve in the ground and become earth again. That's a new kind of archaeology, of cultural resource management, which I find attractive. Perhaps only some sites should be studied, and others left to live differently in the mind. This might shock friends like Steve Lekson. I know his arguments, and I agree with many of them. We have a lively discussion in which I play both parts. In these ways I am learning about myself.

Our country is one of the few which does not protect cultural resources on private land. Nations as diverse as Mexico and England assume that archaeology is part of the common good. Important sites—rock art, ruins, mounds, earthworks—belong to no one in particular, to everyone in general. Americans, of course, have fierce views on the sanctity of private property rights. Like grizzled wolverines, we hold on to that legbone. Laws now protect human and cultural remains on federal and Indian land. Many states also ensure that a landowner no longer owns the bones or burial goods that came with his or her deed. Beyond that, if it's on your property, you can blow it up, level it, or paint it blue. We are free to rampage through the house of our grandmother.

"Americans are newcomers," Roger Anyon explains. "They don't have a long involved relationship with the land. The linkage just isn't there. Instead there's all this fragmentation, subdividing the land into little pieces. It's a parochial view of the world. There's an attitude in Anglo society of take, take, take. Eventually you have to give back. . . . There's a lot of greed, a lot of greed, and a lot of racism against Indians. In pothunting the motive is usually money. But somewhere behind this, I think, is the notion that if we wipe out all these traces of people who have been here before, then we won't have to acknowledge any of their claims. Manifest Destiny. It's an underlying theme."

I see Roger's point. But it's not the whole story. Ultimately pothunting is fueled by the desire to connect with the past by buying it. There are larger issues of materialism and alienation. Do we feel so separate now that we can put everything—time, history, the whole world—in our pocket?

Certainly the way we respond to a potsherd on the ground reflects our sense of cultural heritage. For non-Indians there must be the recognition of difference, of those who were here then and who are here now. At the same time we are also touching our own tribal self, a shared past of evolution and migration. We are holding something made of the land we have made our home.

When Larry Zimmerman and Roger Anyon point to the racism in their profession, they are right to do so. But if I thought archaeology were inherently racist, I would not be writing a book about it. American archaeology is grounded in the belief that our national heritage extends back thousands of years, that we are deeply, truly multicultural and multiracial.

How we manage cultural resources can be compared to how we manage other resources. Scientists are just beginning to trace the interweavings of the natural world. They have returned, roundabout, to a kind of pantheism: the universe conceived as a whole is God. All the parts make up this whole, and all the parts work together. We cannot destroy our rivers and forests, our midges and minnows, without destroying ourselves.

The same may be true of archaeological resources. Our past, present, and future may form a whole, much as they do in a single human life. As a culture, when we sever the connections to our own past, we may be giving up our emotional connection to the future, to the seventh generation to come. We lose our place on the continuum. We are out of context. At this point our mistakes can be profound.

In archaeology, and within archaeology, the acceptance of cultural diversity is an exercise in survival. Diversity appears to be the will of the universe. No war, no form of oppression, can obliterate it. Our instincts tell us to cherish the familiar, that small group bound by trust and blood. Evolution tells us to bloom into difference, a thousand ways of speaking and behaving and seeing the world. Somehow we have to do both. With a network of technology that includes the nuclear bomb, we've invented the oxymoron "global village." Now we have to live in it.

As we hold that potsherd, warm from the sun and gritty with dirt, we have the choice to fill this moment with all the power of our imagination. We can fit into a physical and cultural landscape, finding our place there, enfolded in time. This, of course, is not management at all. It is an embrace.

23328000336600   Anderson, David B.

1) 08 NOV 2005 33328001073051
   The Godfather Part I [videore
   15 NOV 2005 09:00pm

2) 08 NOV 2005 33900000924540
   Never on Sunday [videorecordi
   15 NOV 2005 09:00pm

3) 08 NOV 2005 33328000476271
   Gambler way : Indian gaming i
   29 NOV 2005 09:00pm

4) 08 NOV 2005 33328000838538
   Ojibway heritage
   29 NOV 2005 09:00pm

5) 08 NOV 2005 33328000474359
   When the land was young : ref
   29 NOV 2005 09:00pm

6) 08 NOV 2005 33328000476578
   A simple & informative guide
   29 NOV 2005 09:00pm

7) 08 NOV 2005 33328000183513
   Giving voice to bear : North
   29 NOV 2005 09:00pm

PORT # circ1

EAGLE'S NEST

FROM THE TOP OF THE MESA, THE TRAIL ANGLES
through juniper and scrub brush. I lean back against gravity. My companions are a group of students from the
Crow Canyon Archaeological Center on a tour through
the Ute Mountain Tribal Park. When we first see the cliff
dwelling, set into the brown-and-white bluffs, most of us
fall silent. Like the sighting of some large animal in the
wild, a bear or a mountain lion, the 1,000-year-old ruin
stops my breath. I have a sense of beauty and danger. The
wrong move now might be disastrous.

We are twenty miles southwest of Mesa Verde, with
its larger and more spectacular cliff dwellings. Kim

Malville, a professor of solar astrophysics at the University of Colorado, leads us down the rocky path. Kim points out that archaeology and astronomy are oddly compatible; both look back through time.

In the shade of an overhang, the air is cool and the cliff dwelling seems small, a half-dozen crumbling rooms. We are keenly aware of space and the canyon floor hundreds of feet below. The man next to me blares, "The Anasazi Hilton!" Perhaps he feels embarrassed at entering so brazenly a site hushed, empty, yet clearly someone else's home. Perhaps he simply feels happy on this summer's day surrounded by trees, canyons, mesas, and little else.

Lightly we touch the walls of coursed stone and peer through square windows into a musty darkness. Kim wants to get a few measurements, the angle of light through a certain window. Across the Southwest, architecture deliberately followed the sun, and Kim delights in tracking these relationships, of corners to equinoxes, towers to azimuths. Some of the group are eager to help him. The rest of us stand and sit and peer and walk about, trying to fit this ruin into the story of our lives.

Archaeology is a mirror, and our fascination with cliff dwellings is another reflection. Where I live in New Mexico, over 50,000 people annually visit the Gila Cliff Dwellings National Monument. Yet this forty-room ruin, built by a small group of wandering farmers, was lived in for less than fifty years.

"Cliff dwellings are visually dramatic, and we respond to them for personal and aesthetic reasons," Steve

Lekson reminds me. "But from an archaeologist's point of view, they aren't usually very important."

At the visually dramatic Mesa Verde, millions of people come to stare at villages of mud and stone that seem to float above the valley floor. In the afternoon heat they shimmer like illusions. We have named them from the depth of our Hollywood heart: Sun Temple, Fire Temple, Mummy House, Cliff Palace. Cradled in rock, they evoke a rare serenity. They make us feel less afraid.

Yet "Mesa Verde was marginal." Steve Lekson shrugs. "That's not where the action was."

The action was down in the Montezuma Valley, where a population of 30,000 Anasazi lived in eight scattered settlements that Kim Malville calls "incipient cosmic cities." One of these was Yellow Jacket, a center of 2,500, more than all of Mesa Verde combined. Amid the houses and granaries, over 100 kivas were organized in rows east to west, each associated with a block of rooms. Twenty towers dotted this large complex. A Great Kiva and Great House bordered the north. To the south, monoliths of stone pointed to the summer solstice dawn.

In these forms of ritual Kim sees an "astronomical infrastructure consisting of people with skill, knowledge, and power." Like the Hopewell, the Anasazi were well aware of the major and minor standstills of the moon. They could determine the cardinal directions and align their buildings to match the stars. Horizon calendars used local landmarks and the changing position of sunrise and moonrise to predict solstices and equinoxes. Other calendars were created in architecture and rock art.

The farmers at Yellow Jacket dug fields for corn and squash. Their lives depended on the right number of frost-free days. Still, skywatching was more than a way to determine planting dates. On a certain June morning, for example, the sun rises behind a jagged formation called Lizard Head. As the star climbs the peak, it appears for a moment to be viciously stabbed. Kim wonders "what stories may have grown up around that astronomical event . . . the encounter with Lizard Head may have been viewed in local myth as one of those challenges and tests which the sun had to undergo each year." From this point on, sixteen days remain until actual solstice, time enough to gather the dancers and make food.

Because the Anasazi were such close observers, Kim believes they must have been alarmed around A.D. 1200, when a period of sunspot activity reached its peak. Visible to the naked eye, dark blotches now disfigured the sun. In humans, malignant melanomas may have increased. Climate patterns also began to change, with increasing periods of drought and cold. By A.D. 1300 the Anasazi had abandoned the entire San Juan River drainage. They did not mysteriously disappear. But in a massive migration they moved suddenly and quickly, south to the lands of the historic Hopi, Zuni, and Rio Grande pueblos. At archaeological conferences the question of why is still debated.

Not an archaeologist, Kim freely pursues his favorite theory. "Much of what drove the Anasazi astronomer," he writes, "may have been stimulated by the unstable climate associated with the Medieval Maximum of sunspot activity.

We can speculate on the thoughts of the priests, observing the sun through the morning mists with puzzlement and horror. Ominous black spots crawled across its surface, the land was cold and dry, and society was falling apart. The dark side of Father Sun has asserted itself, and beneath the flecked sun the people said, 'We must flee.' "

OUR GROUP CONTINUES, past this first cliff dwelling, up to Eagle's Nest. To reach that smaller ruin we must climb a long and seemingly vertical pole ladder. After that a second trail defines the line between air and cliff. We ascend to stone rooms perched defiantly, literally, like the nests of birds.

Far below me I can see the spidery vein of canyons entering into a deeper canyon winding north. I can see for nearly 100 miles, all of it harsh, dry, uninhabited country: jumbled hills, rock faces, volcanic debris. The thin layer of organic life is a coat of blurred green, patchy and worn, easily stripped away.

"How far to the bottom?" someone asks.

"Far enough," Kim says.

One member of our group is a teenaged boy. "I'd never live here!" he exclaims in horror. "What if you got drunk or something?"

My response, too, is subjective. I see babies, toddlers, children dashing off to play. "You couldn't raise a family," I murmur.

Standing on a ledge in a stone room, we speculate what people did do here. Perhaps they climbed so high out of fear or paranoia. Perhaps they were priests or social outcasts, hermits, astronomers, misanthropes, criminals, leaders.

Breathing hard, I blink at a view that is too big and too indifferent. Again I have a sense of danger. My bones yearn to elongate and grow hollow. They whisper the false remembrance of flight. Yes, that would be a fine intoxication.

I understand here how easy it is to die. I am, in fact, only a step away. Archaeology, I realize, is about death. This place, I intuit, Eagle's Nest, was also about death, transcendence, and renewal.

The spirit of the cliff dwelling expands to the horizon, large enough to fill this view: the deaths of all who lived here before, the death I will someday know, the deaths of my children, the rise and fall of generations, and of generations after them. Here, so clearly, death is flight. Consciousness fluttering at the pane of the world. The spread of wings lifting.

We forget too often the power of what we are. We forget that awe is one of our gifts.

I stand on a ledge in a stone room. People wait behind me, and eventually I must turn around, back down the narrow trail, back down the pole ladder. With relief and regret I feel its smoothness, the polished wood under my hand. As I leave, part of me believes that this is my real home. Part of me believes I should stay.

It is something I can hold, something to keep.

NOTES

HOUSE OF MIRRORS

The quotes from Bruce Trigger are from his book *A History of Archaeological Thought* (Cambridge University Press, 1989). Another good source for this section is *Processual and Postprocessual Archaeology: Multiple Ways of Knowing the Past* (Center for Archaeological Investigations, 1991), edited by Robert W. Preucel.

The material from Patty Jo Watson is from personal interviews, as well as from the article "The Razor's Edge: Symbolic Structuralist Archaeology and the Expansion of Archaeological Inference," by Patty Jo Watson and Michael Fotiadis, in *American Anthropology* 92 (3), September 1990.

The quote from Claude Lévi-Strauss is cited in Margrit Eichler and Jeanne Lapointe's *On the Treatment of the Sexes in Research* (Social Sciences and Humanities Research Council of Canada, 1985), page 11.

Margaret Conkey's remarks are from her preface to *Engendering Archaeology: Women and Prehistory* (Basil Blackwell, 1993), edited by Margaret Conkey and Joan Gero. The book also contains Joan Gero's paper "Genderlithics: Women's Roles in Stone Tool Production."

The panel of Native American archaeologists were at the forum titled "Native Americans, Archaeologists, and Sacred Places" at the 1994 SAA conference in Anaheim.

The prices of marketed artifacts are from "Is America Allowing Its Past to be Stolen?" by Robert Landers, in *Congressional Quarterlies Editorial Research Reports,* January 18, 1991.

EMOTIONAL BAGGAGE

An excellent discussion on first settlement is David Meltzer's *Search for the First Americans* (Smithsonian Institution Press, 1993). Also, *The First Americans: Search and Research* (CRC Press, 1991), edited by Tom Dillehay and David Meltzer.

Vance Haynes's quotes and related material are from personal interviews, as well as articles and papers. A good general essay is his "Geofacts and Fancy," *National History,* February 1988.

David Whitley's quotes and related material are from personal interviews and correspondence, as well as articles and papers. Specifically, his article, written with Ronald I. Dorn, "New Perspectives on the Clovis versus Pre-Clovis Controversy" in *American Antiquity* 58 (4), 1993.

James Adovasio's quotes and related material are from personal interviews, as well as articles and papers. A good general summary is his essay "Pennsylvania Pioneers," *Natural History,* December 1986. Also, "The Meadowcroft Rockshelter Radiocarbon Chronology 1975–1990," *American Antiquity* 55 (2), 1990.

Tom Dillehay's quotes and related material are from personal interviews, as well as articles and papers. A good general essay is his "By the Banks of Chinchihuapi," *Natural History,* April 1987. Also, his book *Monte Verde: A Late Pleistocene Settlement in Chile, Volume I* (Smithsonian Institution Press, 1993).

Vance Haynes's last quote is from his article "Clovis Origin Update," *The Kiva* 55 (2), 1987.

I also benefited from subscribing to the quarterly *Mammoth Trumpet* (Center for the Study of the First Americans, Oregon State University.)

CLOVISIA THE BEAUTIFUL

Paul Martin's quotes and related material are from personal interviews, as well as articles and papers. A good overview can be found in his book, coedited with Richard S. Klein, *Quaternary Extinctions: A Prehistoric Revolution* (University of Arizona Press, 1984).

Don Grayson's quotes and related material are from personal interviews, as well as articles and papers. This topic and others are covered in his book *The Desert's Past: A Natural Prehistory of the Great Basin* (Smithsonian Institution Press, 1993).

Jared Diamond discusses the loss of Pleistocene animals and its impact on world history in his "Why was Post-Pleistocene Development of Human Societies Slightly More Rapid in the Old World than in the New World?" in *Americans Before Columbus: Ice Age Origins* (University of Pittsburgh, 1988), edited by Ronald Carlisle. Edward Wilson also mentions the controversy of Pleistocene extinctions in his *The Diversity of Life* (Harvard University Press, 1994).

Joanne Dickenson's quotes and related material are from personal interviews, as well as articles and papers. More information can be found in *Clovis: Origins and Adaptations* (Center for the Study of the First Americans, 1991), edited by Robson Bonnichsen and Karen L. Turnmire. George Frison and others have written about the experimental use of Clovis weapons on elephants.

Robin Fox's quote is from his *The Search for Society: Quest for a Biosocial Science and Morality* (Rutgers University Press, 1989).

WOMEN'S WORK

The quotes from Glen Doran and related material are from personal interviews, as well as articles and papers. A good overview is "Multidisciplinary Investigations at the Windover Site" in *Wetsite Archaeology* (Telford Press, 1988), edited by Barbara A. Purdy. Also, *The Art and Archaeology of Florida's Wetlands* (CRC Press, 1991) by Barbara Purdy.

The quote from Cecil Antone is from *Preservation on the Reservation: Native Americans, Native American Lands,*

and Archaeology (Navajo Nation Archaeology Department, 1990), edited by Anthony Klesert and Alan S.
Downer.

Patty Jo Watson's quotes and related material are
from personal interviews, as well as articles and papers. In
particular, her "A Parochial Primer: The New Dissonance as Seen from the Midcontinental U.S." in *Processual
and Postprocessual Archaeology: Multiple Ways of Knowing the
Past* (Center for Archaeological Investigations, 1991), edited by Robert Preucel. Also, *The Origins of Agriculture:
An International Perspective* (Smithsonian Institution Press,
1992), edited by Wesley Cowan and Patty Jo Watson,
which includes Bruce Smith's essay "Prehistoric Plant
Husbandry in Eastern North America."

The quote on the use of bottle gourds by male shamans is from "The Origins of Plant Domestication in the
Eastern United States: Promoting the Individual in Archaeological Theory" by Guy Prentice in *Southeastern Archaeology* 5, 1986.

Bruce Smith's quotes are from his "Reconciling the
Gender-credit Critique and the Floodplain Weed Theory
of Plant Domestication" in *Archaeological Reports,* Number 25, 1993.

For a discussion of feminism see *Engendering Archaeology: Women and Prehistoy* (Basil Blackwell, 1993), edited by
Margaret Conkey and Joan Gero. Also, Margaret Conkey
and Sarah H. Williams's paper "Original Narrative: The
Political Economy of Gender in Archaeology" in *Gender at
the Crossroads of Knowledge: Feminist Anthropology in the
Postmodern Era* (University of California Press, 1991). I also

cite Joan Gero's work "Socio-Politics and the Woman-at-Home Ideology" in *American Antiquity* 50 (2), 1985.

COUNTDOWN

Two good general books on ancient America are *Ancient North America* (Thames and Hudson, 1991) by Brian Fagan and *Prehistory of the Americas* (Cambridge University Press, 1992) by Stuart J. Fiedel.

Dale Croes's quotes and related material are from personal interviews, as well as articles and papers. In particular, "Hoko River Archaeological Complex: Modeling Prehistoric Northwest Coast Economic Evolution" by Dale Croes and Steven Hackenberger in *Research in Economic Anthropology* 3, 1988. Also, *The Hoko River Archaeological Site Complex* (Washington State University, 1995) by Dale Croes.

I also cite Allen W. Johnson and Timothy Earle's *The Evolution of Human Societies: From Foraging Group to Agrarian State* (Stanford University Press, 1987).

The comment on Big Men as functional or fungal is from Gary Coupland's "Prehistoric Economic and Social Change in the Tsimshian Area" in *Research in Economic Anthropology* (Jai Press, 1988), edited by Barry Issac.

A good general book is *Tradition and Change on the Northwest Coast* (University of Washington Press, 1986) by Ruth Kirk, which is also the source of her quote on slavery.

Todd Bostwick's quotes and related material are from personal interviews, as well as articles and papers. In particular, his "Platform Mound Ceremonialism in Southern Arizona" in *Proceedings of the Second Salado Conference* (Arizona Archaeological Society, 1992), edited by Richard C. Lange and Stephen Germick.

A good general book is *The Hohokam: Ancient People of the Desert* (School of American Research, 1991), edited by David Grant Noble.

David Carrasco discusses concepts of world centering and world making in his *Religions of MesoAmerica: Cosmovision and Ceremonial Centers* (Harpers San Francisco, 1990).

Brad Lepper's quotes and related material are from personal interviews, as well as articles and papers. In particular, "The Newark Earthworks and the Geometric Enclosures of Scioto, Ohio: Connections and Conjectures." Also, *Vanishing Heritage* (Licking County Archaeology and Landscape Society, 1992), edited by Paul E. Hooge and Bradley T. Lepper.

Bruce Trigger's quote is from his *A History of Archaeological Thought* (Cambridge University Press, 1989).

The quote on Bruce Trigger's story of nineteenth-century scholars is from "Methodological Impacts of Catastrophic Depopulation on American Archaeology and Ethnology" by Robert C. Dunnell in *Columbian Consequences, Volume 3,* edited by David Hurst Thomas (Smithsonian Press, 1991).

BRIGHT LIGHTS, BIG CITY

A good source on Cahokia is *Cahokia: City of the Sun* (Cahokia Mounds Museum Society, 1992).

Also, Lynda Norene Shaffer's *Native Americans Before 1492: The Moundbuilding Centers of the Eastern Woodlands* (Sharpe, 1992). The quote from Tattoed Serpent's wife is in this book, as well as in Charles M. Hudson's *The Southeastern Indians* (University of Tennessee, 1976).

Steve Lekson's quotes and related material are from personal interviews, as well as articles and papers. In particular, "Mimbres Art and Archaeology" in *Archaeology, Art, and Anthropology: Papers in Honor of J.J. Brody* (The Archaeological Society of New Mexico, 1992), edited by Meliha S. Duran and David Kirkpatrick and "Cognitive Frameworks and Chacoan Architecture" in *New Mexico Journal of Science* 21 (1), June 1981. Also, "The Chaco Canyon Community, with cowriters Thomas C. Winder, John R. Stein, and W. James Judge, in *Scientific American,* Volume 259, Number 1, July 1988. Another good essay by Steve on Chaco Canyon is in *Chaco Canyon: A Center and its World* (Museum of New Mexico Press, 1994).

FIRST CONTACT

A good general source on first contact in Florida is *First Encounters: Spanish Explorations in the Caribbean and the United States* (University of Florida Press, 1989), edited by Jerald T. Milanich and Susan Milbrath.

Quotes from Cabeza de Vaca are taken from *Cabeza de Vaca's Adventures in the Unknown Interior of America* (University of New Mexico Press, 1992), translated by Cyclone Covey. Another good translation is *The Account: Álvar Núñez Cabeza de Vaca's Relación* (Arte Publico Press, 1993), translated by Martin A. Favata and Jose B. Fernandez.

Rochelle Marrinan's quotes and related material are from personal interviews, as well as papers and articles. In particular, her "Prelude to de Soto: The Expedition of Panfilo de Narváez," written with John F. Scarry and Rhonda L. Majors, in *Columbian Consequences, Volume 3* (Smithsonian Institution Press, 1991), edited by David Hurst Thomas.

The quote on cubist perspective is from David Hurst Thomas's preface "Columbian Consequences: the Spanish Borderlands in Cubist Perspective" in *Columbian Consequences, Volume 1* (Smithsonian Institution Press, 1990), edited by David Hurst Thomas.

Kathleen Deagan's quotes and related material are from personal interviews, as well as articles and papers. In particular, her paper "The Emergence of a Multi-Cultural Society: Spanish America After 1492," presented at the 24th annual meeting of the Society for Historical Archaeology, January 1992. Also, her "Spanish-Indian Interaction in 16th Century Florida and Hispaniola" in *Cultures in Contact* (Smithsonian Institution Press, 1985), edited by William Fitzhugh.

Rolena Adorno's material comes from her articles "The Discursive Encounter of Spain and America: The Authority of Eyewitness Testimony in the Writing of History" in *William and Mary Quarterly* and "The Negotiation of Fear in Cabeza de Vaca's *Naufragios*" in *Representations* 33, Winter 1991.

The quote on despair and depopulation is from David E. Stannard's chapter "The Consequences of Contact: Toward an Interdisciplinary Theory of Native Responses to Biological and Cultural Invasion" in *Columbian*

Conseqences, Volume 3 (Smithsonian Institution Press, 1991), edited by David Hurst Thomas.

A GOOD WISH

Roger Echo-Hawk's quotes and related material are from personal interviews, as well as articles and papers. A good book on the subject of reburial is *Battlefields and Burial Grounds: The Indian Struggle to Protect Ancestral Graves in the United States* (Lerner Publications, 1994) by Roger C. Echo-Hawk and Walter R. Echo-Hawk. This includes the quotes from James Fenimore Cooper and from the Nebraska museum director. Also, Roger's thesis *Kara Katit Pakutu: Exploring the Origins of Native America in Anthropology and Oral Traditions,* submitted to the University of Colorado, 1994.

Larry Zimmerman's quotes and related material are from personal interviews, as well as articles and papers. In particular, his "The Past is a Foreign Country," the 40th Annual Harrington Lecture, College of Arts and Sciences, University of South Dakota and "Archaeology, Reburial, and the Tactics of a Discipline's Self-delusion" in *American Indian Culture and Research Journal* 16 (2), 1992. Also, "Made Radical by my Own: an archaeologist learns to accept reburial" in *Conflict in the Archaeology of Living Traditions* (Unwin Hyman, 1989), edited by Robert Layton and "The Crow Creek Experience" in *Early Man,* Autumn 1981.

The quotes from Maria D. Pearson, Cecil Antone, and Ben Rhodd are from *Preservation on the Reservation: Native Americans, Native American Lands, and Archaeology*

(Navajo Nation Archaeology Department, 1990), edited by Anthony Klesert and Alan S. Downer.

Jan Hammil-BearShield's quote is from "Statement of American Indians Against Desecration before the World Archaeological Congress" in *Conflict in the Archaeology of Living Traditions* (Unwin Hyman, 1989), edited by Robert Layton.

Lynne Goldstein's quote is from "The Potential for Future Relationships between Archaeologists and Native Americans" in *Quandaries and Quests: Visions of Archaeology's Future* (Center for Archaeological Investigations, 1992), edited by Lu Ann Wandsnider.

Clement Meighan's first quote is from "Another View on Repatriation: Lost to the Public, Lost to History" in *The Public Historian* 14 (3), Summer 1992. His comment on the Idaho reburial comes from "A famous skeleton returns to the earth" by Samantha Silva, *High Country News,* March 8, 1993.

Larry Benallie's quotes and related material come from personal interviews, as well as articles and papers.

Davina TwoBears's quotes are from "A Navajo Student's Perception: Anthropology and the Navajo Nation Archaeology Department Student Training Program" in the *Society for American Archaeology Bulletin* 13 (1), January/ February 1995.

Roger Anyon's quotes and related material are from personal interviews, as well as articles and papers.

IN OUR GRANDMOTHER'S HOUSE

Cathy Cameron's quotes and related material are from personal interviews, as well as articles and papers. In particular, her "The Destruction of the Past: Nonrenewable Cultural Resources" in *Nonrenewable Resources* 3 (1), Spring 1994.

Lynn Teague's quotes and related material are from personal interviews, as well as articles and papers.

Allen Funkhouser's quotes and related material are from personal interviews, as well as articles and papers.

The quote from the Utah state archaeologist David Madson to a congressional subcommittee is from "Is America Allowing Its Past to be Stolen?" by Robert Landers, in *Congressional Quarterlies Editorial Research Reports,* January 18, 1991.

The quote on the hypocrisy of our standards in marketing artifacts is from Thomas F. King in "Some Dimensions of the Pothunting Problem" in *Protecting the Past* (CRC Press, 1991), edited by George S. Smith and John R. Ehrenhad. The introduction to *Protecting the Past* contains some statistics on the status of looted sites in America.

The quotes from the National Park Service archaeologist who worked in a sting operation are from "Project Sting" by John Neary in *Archaeology,* September/October 1993. This is also the source for some statistics on the status of looted sites on public land (originally taken from a 1987 General Accounting Office report).

EAGLE'S NEST

Kim Malville's quotes and related material are from personal interviews, as well as articles and papers. In particular, *Prehistoric Astronomy in the Southwest* (Johnson Books, 1993) by J. McKim Malville and Claudia Putnam.

INDEX

221